EVIDENCE NO. AP4421-99X2-2641

CHAIN OF CUSTODY

- Received from: Gov. Vaxvissh Kal Ness//By: Maj. Heck Ensio//
  - Received from: Maj. Heck Ensio//By: Master Archivist Mordianius//
    - Received from: Master Archivist Mordianius//By: Korr Sella//

ATTN: GENERAL LEIA ORGANA
FROM: KORR SELLA

As discussed, please find the artifact recovered from the excavation on Durkteel. While clearing ground for a comm tower, the crew broke into a buried chamber filled with dirt and what appeared to be a number of old war relics. They called in the bomb squad, who retrieved an armored case in question and sent it to the planetary governor, which eventually made its way to me.

The case bore Rebel Alliance identifiers. Its contents were intended to be viewed only by senior members of Alliance High Command. You're one of the only people who still fits that description.

CONTEXT RE: ARTIFACT DISCOVERY

Durkteel's records from the Galactic Civil War are practically nonexistent. Fortunately, we have Imperial service records from the same period and have pinpointed the action we believe caused the loss of this particular artifact.

Occurring on the same day as the Battle of Endor, three Star Destroyers positioned themselves above the outskirts of Durkteel's industrial center in response to rumors of a secret rebel meeting. After jamming transmissions, the Empire chose not to make arrests or demand surrender. Instead, they went straight to orbital bombardment.

Several artifacts have been recovered from the site, but only this vault has been deemed to possess significant military or intelligence value.

It seems clear that the rebels weren't prepared for the Empire's response, and also that someone wanted to preserve the information inside this collection.

Please review, and bring in additional perspectives on this material where appropriate. These secrets haven't been read for thirty years. Something feels good about finally giving them back their voices.

THE REBEL FILES

COLLECTED INTELLIGENCE OF THE ALLIANCE

SHELL TOP-LEVEL/CATEGORY

ALLIANCE CHRON 1

ABSTRACT:

Organizing the Rebellion

Hendri Underholt

ARCHIVIST

STANDARD DATE: 14-17 AFE

(AFTER THE FORMATION OF THE EMPIRE)

In addition to wiping away the Republic, the Emperor reset the dating system to the time before the formation of the Empire and the time after its formation—yet another display of his absolute control.

—Leia

MON MOTHMA

Hendri, I am entrusting you with maintaining a central data repository concerning the most sensitive information on the formation of the Rebellion and related operations.

HENDRI UNDERHOLT

Senator, I'm honored.

MON MOTHMA

One copy, nonelectronic, to be stored in a code-locked case armed with destructive safeguards.

We seem to have bypassed the worst of these. Fortunate that we were able to recover the contents at all. -EMATT

HENDRI UNDERHOLT

I . . . oh fates.
Are you sure you wouldn't rather have Erskin do this?
Or Hostis?
Or Auxy?

MON MOTHMA

Any of them would do a fine job. So will you. You're on my staff now. In this job you'll encounter people who will try to minimize you. Don't do their work for them.

MOTHMA | JOURNAL ENTRY

I have fought this battle for nearly two decades, starting even before Palpatine declared himself Emperor of the galaxy. I always recognized the danger he presented, but I clearly underestimated the scope of his greed.

The Republic Senate is now the Imperial Senate, and I still represent the people of Chandrila. Yet what power do I actually wield in that role? What check does a legislature have against a dictator?

All is not lost in the Senate. I believe that Palpatine started his career there. It is an institution with centuries of history. As long as it exists, it puts a face to the Emperor's political opposition.

Other measures are needed. We must also fight through force of arms. Palpatine's militarization will flatten the resistance unless we bare our teeth.

CONTINUED

Even a behemoth will shudder when it bleeds from a thousand bites.

Bail and I lead double lives. We demonstrate principled dissension in front of the holocams while organizing paramilitary raids from the shadows.

The organization we've built is not the only rebel network. If we can combine these scattered cells—linking our communications, sharing our resources, hitting the same targets at the same time—we could topple Palpatine from his Coruscant throne.

If not, Imperial Intelligence will expose each cell and the Emperor's star fleet will throttle us one by one. We must unite or die.

At the end, my father barely hid his contempt, even during Senate sessions. If he had gone underground, he may have survived. But we didn't know how despicable Tarkin could be.
—Leia

Unifying the galaxy's rebel factions sounds wise, but I've served on too many Senate subcommittees to expect a smooth road. Egos, infighting, and tribalism will fracture any partnership.

The Rebellion requires both political and paramilitary leadership. I believe this structure is scalable as our assets and allies grow.

Political High Command

Chief of State

Minister of Finance	Minister of Education	Minister of State
Minister of Industry	Minister of Supply	Minister of War

In shaping the resistance I have cut the political organ almost entirely. But of course the New Republic already has a Senate, helpless as it is. What it needs are fighters.
—Leia

After a lifetime as a senator, it says something that I'll be remembered as a general?
—Leia

CONTINUED

NOT BY ACCIDENT, THIS MIMICS THE STRUCTURE OF A CIVIL GOVERNMENT. ONE DAY—FORCE WILLING—THIS IS HOW WE WILL GOVERN THE GALAXY.

Wise words, and so early in the Alliance's fleet buildup! Admiral Ackbar

THE SUCCESSFUL INTEGRATION OF THE ATRIVIS CELL INTO OUR STRUCTURE IS A SIGN THAT THIS HIERARCHY IS BROADLY FUNCTIONAL.

As of yet, however, none of the Mon Cal city-ships had been converted for combat. -Statura

MILITARY HIGH COMMAND

COMMANDER IN CHIEF

FLEET COMMAND	STARFIGHTER COMMAND	SECTOR COMMAND	INTELLIGENCE

SPECIAL FORCES	ORDNANCE AND SUPPLY	SUPPORT SERVICES

SLUGGING MATCHES WITH THE IMPERIAL NAVY WILL BENEFIT NO ONE. ON THE OTHER HAND, WHY BUILD A FLEET AND NOT USE IT?

Well, of course they hadn't! I was there. Admiral Ackbar

I REMEMBER THE TALKS AT CANTHAM HOUSE WITH BAIL, IN THOSE FIRST YEARS UNDER THE NEW REGIME. WE'VE COME SO FAR FROM HUSHED HYPOTHETICALS.

BAIL ORGANA TO MON MOTHMA

Rebel Intelligence is identifying more resistance cells every day. Our strategy is to observe them from a distance. If they demonstrate competency at disrupting Imperial operations and remaining hidden, we will reach out. If they don't, we must leave them to their fate.

Cruel, but it serves our cause. When the Empire cracks down on amateurs, it convinces the moffs that they're getting results and hitting the right targets. Meanwhile, we gain time to grow.

Which is a roundabout way of asking, what should we do with Gerrera's Partisans? Pushing away troublesome potential allies is what the Empire *wants* us to do. The Rebellion can't afford to be at war with itself.

We don't have to approve of Saw's methods, but compromise can sometimes be in the service of a larger good.

I remember Saw. Bloviators liked to debate whether Saw's approach was tolerable or inexcusable, but Mon Mothma made her opinion clear. Leia

I KNEW HIM MORE BY REPUTATION. ONE OF MY SCOUTS SERVED WITH THE PARTISANS, AND SHE TURNED OUT OKAY. -EMATT

MON MOTHMA TO BAIL ORGANA

You were always closer to the Jedi than I, but there was something I admired about their purity. For the Jedi, compromising any moral principle led to the dark side. And therefore, they never compromised. Not with lives, and not so casually. At first it seems unconscionable to plan military missions knowing people on both sides will die. Over time it becomes easier and easier until you feel a numb nothingness.

Saw is too far gone, Bail. Victory at any cost is no victory.

BORMEA TODAY

DATE 8 YEARS BFE

WIZARD! TEEN SENATOR TAKES ON CORUSCANT

SALLINE, CHANDRILA—*Bormea Today* secured an exclusive one-on-one with local sensation Mon Mothma, the teenaged go-getter who's sure to shake up the Republic Senate with her smiles and sass!

BORMEA TODAY: We're so excited to talk to you, and our readers can't wait to get to know you better!

MON MOTHMA: Thank you. I'm fortunate and grateful to be in this position.

BT: The new legislative session starts in less than a week. Are you nervous about meeting the chief of state?

MM: More eager than nervous. I plan to take the chief of state through the three elements of my plan for improving the lives of the people in the Bormea sector: investment in infrastructure, decreased corporatism, and equal representation for both colonists and homeworlders.

BT: Exciting stuff! Moving on, a reader from Ganthel writes, "Mon Mothma, who's your favorite Core Drive musician?"

I'm not surprised in the least. —Leia

Even under the New Republic, nothing has changed. And yet the holonet continues to ask why I'm such a private individual. —Holdo

TO: Senator Leia Organa
FROM: Senator Mon Mothma

Leia,
Congratulations on your appointment as junior senator for the Alderaan sector. I'm tempted to say I know what it's like to be in your shoes, but the galaxy has changed dramatically since my election.

Because you're young, you possess idealism and drive in vast quantities. They are precious resources. Use them now. It's a little-discussed secret that both of these traits come with expiration dates. When you get to be my age, you'll find that most of your peers tossed them out long ago.

Your fire is needed now more than ever. Don't allow others to push you from your path. Love who you are, and if you don't, find the strength to start over.

The galaxy needs defenders, Leia. Never stop fighting.

Mon Mothma

When I paged to this document my breath seized and I had to blink back tears. I have this same document. A hard copy which I've kept close to me for more than thirty-five years. To learn that she valued it too, enough to preserve it . . . —Leia

DOC #03201194-ALL

TO: CMDR. MOTHMA
FROM: MAJ. HEXTROPHON
SUBJ: "OFFICIAL HISTORY OF THE REBEL MOVEMENTS, VOLUME ONE"

Commander, enclosed are selections from my latest research. I am particularly interested in how the Jedi helped foment local rebellions on Separatist-controlled worlds. As always, I welcome your input.

Also, Lt. Na'al would like to set up an interview with you. He's been a tremendous help, but I'm beginning to suspect he's writing his own book on the side.

Is this Voren? —Holdo

Indeed. The New Republic historian had humble beginnings, it seems. —Statura

He's already booked my schedule for a two-hour lunch the next time he's on D'Qar. Hasn't changed a bit. —Holdo

CONTINUED

TRINEBULON NEWS

The Truth, Straight from the Source

SYNDULLA STRIKES AGAIN

Kala'uun, Ryloth—Imperial loyalists condemned the Free Ryloth movement after outlaw Cham Syndulla claimed responsibility for a reservoir explosion that washed away an Imperial hovertrain.

"Since the Clone Wars, Syndulla and his raiders have selfishly claimed dominion over Ryloth, in defiance of Imperial law and the wishes of its people," said Governor Pommel. "I call upon Syndulla to surrender or face obliteration."

During the Clone Wars, Syndulla willingly accepted arms and training from Jedi agents in exchange for fighting the Separatist occupiers. The defeat of the Separatists did not stop Syndulla, who continued his raids against the planet's Imperial liberators.

(see p. 2)

TriNeb, the only news outlet still willing to shill for the First Order.
—Holdo

CONTINUED

CYNABAR'S INFONET

Always Bet on the Big CYN

The Arkanis sector—Someone's making life miserable for the territorial moff, and this time it's not Syndulla.

The Partisans have scored a number of wins against Imperial storehouses, convoys, and inspection stations, leaving no survivors. It's a rare display of ruthlessness from the growing anti-Empire resistance.

The Partisans are led by Saw Gerrera, an ex-Onderon freedom fighter with a hefty bounty on his head. After these attacks that bounty is only going to increase, so hunters willing to be patient might get a bigger payout.

CONTINUED

DOC #0320194-ALL

MEETING MINUTES: CANTHAM HOUSE TALKS
INVITEES: LOYALIST COMMITTEE MEMBERS AND SELECTED SENATORS
SUBJECT: PETITION OF 2,000

BAIL ORGANA (ALDERAAN): Thank you all for attending. I know we can count on the signatures, but I've invited this group to discuss the exact wording of the petition.

MON MOTHMA (CHANDRILA): In broad strokes, our demands are that Chancellor Palpatine relinquish the emergency war powers granted to him, abolish the Sector Governance Decree, and begin cease-fire talks with Count Dooku's Separatists.

TERR TANEEL (SENEX): [with that last point] Are we going too far? The war is popular in my sector. We would be seen by many as obstructing an inevitable victory.

PADMÉ AMIDALA (NABOO): People are dying, Senator. The longer this conflict drags out, the more loopholes Palpatine will find for amending the constitution.

Recorded weeks before her death. Who would my mother have become under the revolution? —Leia

DATE 1 DAY AFE

HOLONET NEWS

63 SENATORS ARRESTED IN COLLUSION WITH JEDI INSURGENCY

Imperial City, Coruscant—Imperial Intelligence scored a dramatic victory against the Jedi rebellion today, arresting sixty-three senators on charges of conspiracy and treason. Among those arrested were a number of senators from prominent Core Worlds, as well as many alien senators from Outer Rim worlds.

Only a partial list of the senators involved had been released as of press time.

Among the names released were:

Many of my peers in the Imperial Senate believed we could bring about more good by working within the system. There's a germ of truth in that. —Leia

CONTINUED

DOC #0320194-ALL

» Shea Sadashassa of Herdessa
» Ivor Drake of Kestos Minor
» Fang Zar of Sern Prime
» Streamdrinker of Tynna
» Tanner Cadaman of Feenix

Bail and I were detained but released after we professed our loyalty. Why do I fight the Empire? One reason is my guilt. —Mothma

All those arrested had also been signatories to the Petition of the 2,000, a formal protest against Palpatine's new system of regional governorship that was signed by two thousand legislators and presented during the last full Senate session.

Is your senator a traitor?

DATE 14 YRS AFE

"LIBERATORS" SEIZE IMPERIAL GARRISON ON MANTOOINE

ISSUE CALL FOR ARMED REBELLION IN ATRIVIS SECTOR

LIBERATORS CRUSHED

IMPERIAL NAVY RESTORES ORDER ON MANTOOINE

CATTA DIONIZE, ON BEHALF OF TRAVIA CHAN

GENERIS STATION

After due deliberation, Madame Chan of the Atrivis Resistance Group agrees to the terms of partnership with Senator Mothma of the Alliance. May our factions be stronger together than apart.

No more Mantooines! Down with the Empire!

END DOCUMENT

MON MOTHMA TO ARHUL HEXTROPHON

Thank you for sending this, Arhul. ARG mentioned in the last piece was one of the first groups to join what I was already calling the "Alliance." A bit of puffery at that stage, but I trust history will excuse it. I expected these materials to be light reading, but they sobered me instead. You made me realize how much work we still have to do.

If only more people recognized the threat of the First Order. Palpatine's reign inspired thousands of revolutionary cells. Right now we're essentially alone and fighting a phantom enemy. —Holdo

CLASSIFIED DOCUMENT—CLEARANCE LEVEL:

CRACKEN/MOTHMA PROG299844

RI 336-IS

IMPLICATIONS OF THE ANTAR ATROCITY

TO: COMMANDER MOTHMA

FROM: GENERAL AIREN CRACKEN, CHIEF OF REBEL INTELLIGENCE

Commander, some history on the Antar Atrocity, if I may.

When Imperial forces under Wilhuff Tarkin punished the world for siding with the Separatists in the Clone Wars, aggression didn't stop with arrests by secret police. Next came executions, and finally massacres.

Yet despite all that, no one would remember it as the Antar Atrocity if it hadn't leaked to the media. (Belated thanks to Berch Teller, ex-Republic Intelligence—a good man but a bit of a pessimist.)

Teller's example proves it's possible to sway public opinion against the Empire's version of events. Atrocities are happening every day. Let's put resources into counterpropaganda.

DOC #0420265-ALL

TO: GENERAL CRACKEN
FROM: COMMANDER MOTHMA
SUBJ: IMPLICATIONS OF THE ANTAR ATROCITY

I agree, the extermination of the Lasat is yet another of this regime's crimes. Senator Pamlo will lead counterpropaganda in conjunction with your team.

Senator Pamlo and I do not see eye to eye on military matters, but she knows how to shape a story. If we can expose the next Antar Atrocity, we may spur sympathy in the Core and wholesale defections in the Rim.

THE NEW REPUBLIC CONTROLS THE HOLONET. THEY'RE ON "OUR" SIDE BUT UNWILLING TO HEAR US OUT. HOW DO WE GET OUR STORY OUT TO THE GALAXY? – EMATT

CLASSIFIED DOCUMENT—CLEARANCE LEVEL:

TANO/DRAVEN PROG300154

RI 345-X6
LOTHAL RESISTANCE CELL
TO: GENERAL DRAVEN
FROM: AHSOKA TANO

We're making progress on Hosnian Prime and elsewhere. Force help me, it would be so much easier fight the enemy if our allies weren't in the way. –Leia

General,

The Spectres are the real deal. Though small in number, they've executed some big ops thus far:

- rescuing Wookiee prisoners from Kashyyyk
- disabling a Star Destroyer
- disrupting Imperial shipping lines between Lothal and Garel

As previously reported, the Spectre cell includes a Mandalorian saboteur, a Lasat Honor Guard, and an ex-Jedi (see supplemental file on Dume, Caleb). My contact is Spectre One, an ace pilot whose skills are wasted on a VCX-100 freighter (SEE ATTACHED). Imagine what they could do with more hardware and a decent support network.

CONTINUED

SUB THE SPECTRES

SABINE WREN

KANAN JARRUS

EZRA BRIDGER

GARAZEB "ZEB" ORRELIOS

HERA SYNDULLA

C1-10P "CHOPPER"

SURVEILLANCE IMG. 522125-SP
ZOOM: 35X

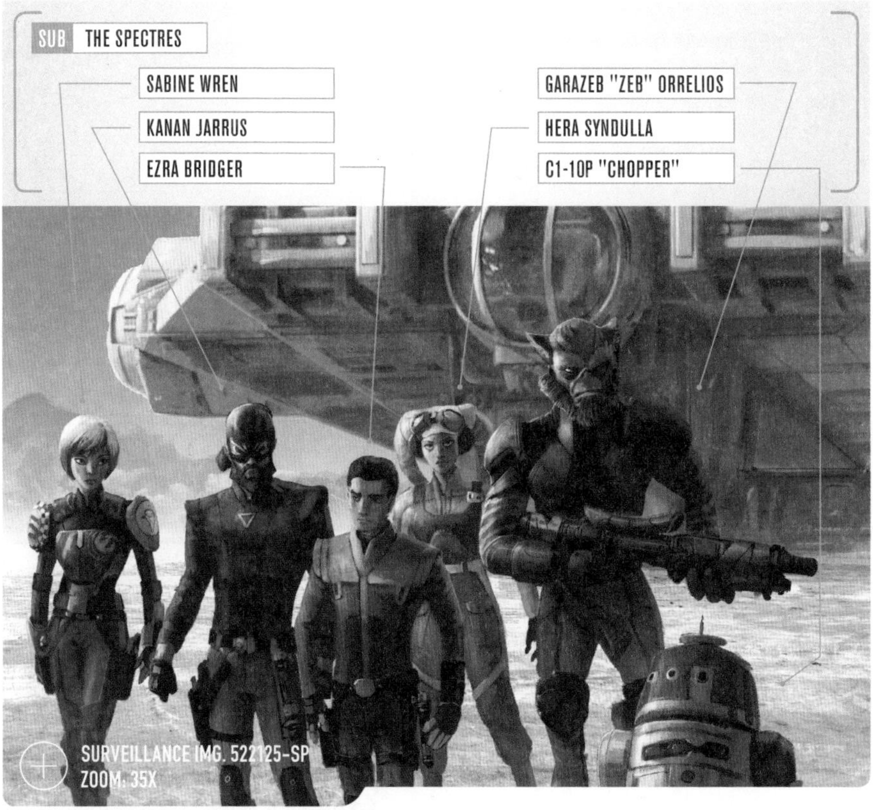

END DOCUMENT

CLASSIFIED DOCUMENT—CLEARANCE LEVEL: 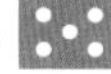

RI 386-IS

INTEL SUMMARY: MAJOR RESISTANCE FACTIONS

TO: COMMANDER MOTHMA

FROM: GENERAL DRAVEN

Commander, please review the following topline (and supplementary datafiles) concerning the major resistance factions active in Imperial space.

CONTINUED

DRAVEN/MOTHMA PROG300653

DATAFILES

PARTISANS

COMMANDER: Saw Gerrera
OPERATIONS: Outer Rim near the Corellian Run

The Partisans have a reputation for ruthlessness, but they get things done. I know that's not what you want to hear, but if we hold back, we'll keep losing ground. We can't afford to remain squeamish.

I could have told them not to swim up current against Faa-Char.
Admiral Ackbar

MON CALS

COMMANDER: Faa-Char
OPERATIONS: Mon Calamari space near Overic Griplink

We enjoy good relations with Raddus and his factions, but the Alliance has yet to convince the bulk of the Mon Cal. In the eyes of the Empire, the actions of Raddus and his Mon Cal refugees have already rendered the entire species guilty of treason. We can help them fight back.

DEEP CURRENT

COMMANDER: Saltbite
OPERATIONS: Tynna, Shipwrights' Trace

Primary an intelligence op, Deep Current has leveraged the Tynnan aptitude for bureaucracy in order to gather voluminous data concerning Imperial Rim deployments and shipyard cargo traffic. If they supply data, we can offer protection.

GUARDIANS OF THE WHILLS

COMMANDER: None
OPERATIONS: Jedha, Freestanding subsectors

Though few of the Guardians have spread offworld, they deserve note for maintaining spiritual opposition to Imperial rule (note potential propaganda value). Guardians possess several esoteric combat traditions. An increased Imperial presence on Jedha has resulted in a stronger garrison in the Holy City and the shuttering of the Temple of the Kyber.

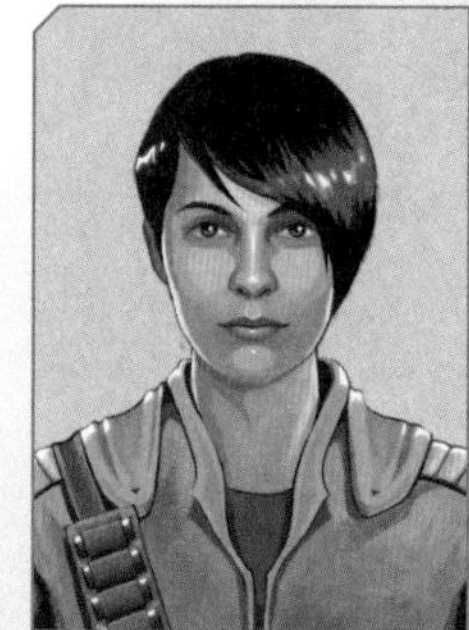

FREEMARCH

COMMANDER: Marilena Pet-and-Ella Alda Mattea
OPERATIONS: Lorrd, Corporate Sector

(see p2)

Is this Deep Fathom?
Admiral Ackbar

CONFIRMED. ONE OF THE RESISTANCE'S BEST RESOURCES FOR INTEL OUT OF THE UNKNOWN REGIONS. STILL UNDER SALTBITE, BUT HE CAN'T SWIM ANYMORE THESE DAYS.
- EMATT

END DOCUMENT

MON MOTHMA TO GEN. DRAVEN

The Partisan group is not good enough, General. They endanger civilians. End of discussion.

CLASSIFIED DOCUMENT—CLEARANCE LEVEL: 

TANO/DRAVEN PROG30954

RI 345-X6

ACTION AT MUSTAFAR

TO: GENERAL DRAVEN

FROM: AHSOKA TANO

General, the Spectres forced our hand at Mustafar, but the incident was a net victory for the Rebellion.

MISSION RECAP: The Spectre cell arrived at Mustafar to rescue one of their own (Kanan Jarrus, see Dume, Caleb) from aboard the ISD *Sovereign*, commanded by Grand Moff Tarkin. After infiltrating, Spectre agents sabotaged the reactor and destroyed the vessel. Tarkin is a confirmed survivor. I led the Alliance sector fleet to Mustafar to cover the Spectres until all units could escape.

POST-MISSION ACTIONS: The Spectres have been integrated into Phoenix cell, reporting to Cmdr. Soto. Spectre leader Hera Syndulla recieved an Alliance officer's commission.

The Hera Syndulla? If only they had known where she'd end up. —Leia

MOTHMA | JOURNAL ENTRY

YES, THE NAVAL ACTION AT MUSTAFAR IS A SHORT-TERM WIN. BUT THE EMPIRE NOW KNOWS THE MEASURE OF THE ALLIANCE'S NAVAL STRENGTH. THE LOSS OF AN IMPERIAL STAR DESTROYER GUARANTEES A SWIFT RESPONSE. THE EMPIRE WILL TIGHTEN SECURITY THROUGHOUT THE OUTER RIM.

THIS MOMENT WAS INEVITABLE, YET I WASN'T PREPARED TO FACE IT SO SOON. THE REBELLION MUST START MAKING AGGRESSIVE MOVES OR WE WILL BE PICKED OFF WHERE WE STAND.

BAIL ORGANA TO MON MOTHMA

Mon—thought you'd enjoy this. The Hammerheads are currently being modified for use by Phoenix squadron.

TO: Moff Stattata, Lothal Sector

FROM: Imperial Senator Leia Organa, Princess of the Royal House of Alderaan

CONCERNING: Gross dereliction of duty

Governor,

I am lodging a formal complaint against the Imperial administration on Lothal. I recently arrived at the capital on a Senate-sponsored relief mission, bringing three ships fully laden with supplies. I repeatedly warned the port commander about ship theft, having been the victim of rebel raids in the past.

Let me state once more: I could not have made my concerns any clearer. Yet despite a landing shackle lockdown and the presence of two patrolling AT-ATs, vile thieves made off with <u>all three ships</u>. Within hours of my arrival!

I demand full Imperial compensation. If this matter is not resolved with the swiftness it deserves, I shall take things up with the Senate.

They paid! Always try everything on the off chance it will actually work.
—Leia

RENUMERATION INVOICE
ATTN: IMPERIAL GOVERNOR, LOTHAL SECTOR

MAKE SETTLEMENT PAYABLE TO: ROYAL HOUSE OF ALDERAAN

Hammerhead corvette *Amity's Arrow*........................650,000 credits
Hammerhead corvette *Lightmaker*..............................650,000 credits
Hammerhead corvette *Duchess Senna*........................650,000 credits
Cargo, relief supplies (68,500 metric tons).................292,500 credits
(see next page for cargo itemization)

OH FATES, NOT BECK! SHE'S THE MONSTER WHO RAN ME TO GROUND ON CYRKON. - EMATT

HENDRI UNDERHOLT

Senator, Agent Beck from the Imperial Security Bureau requested a meeting with you. I lied and said you'd already left Coruscant on a fact-finding mission to Goroth.

MON MOTHMA

Well done, Hendri. Keep the vultures at bay.

DOC #0532286-ALL

TO: CMDR. MOTHMA

FROM: GEN. DODONNA

SUBJ: STARFIGHTER ASSETS

Commander,

I am enclosing reports from our field commanders concerning the Alliance's strongest starfighter assets: the X-wing, the A-wing, the U-wing, and the prototype B-wing.

These starfighters will supplement the Y-wing currently in use. System patrol craft and aging Clone Wars designs (including the rebuilt Delta-7s) are recommended for local engagements only.

CAN'T BELIEVE THEY WERE STILL USING DELTA-7s. MOST CLONE WARS STARFIGHTERS WERE BUILT TOO QUICKLY. DIDN'T HOLD UP TO EXTENDED USE. -POE

If you wish, we can discuss this during your next visit to Dantooine.

COMMANDER JUN SATO TO GENERAL DODONNA

The Rebellion can't ignore the advantage of fast-moving interceptors for hit-and-fade strikes. My unit, Phoenix Squadron, relies heavily on the A-wing and our skilled pilots.

Lacking carriers, we've transported our A-wings aboard a *Pelta*-class frigate and a CR90 corvette (with the help of docking tubes and umbilicals). Dedicated fighter carriers will be required as the Alliance broadens the scope of Starfighter Command.

The A-wing is a single-pilot craft, but we have found the two-seater RZ-1T trainer extremely helpful in certifying bush pilots on the equipment. If models are available, we could use A-wing trainers at the flight schools on Homon and Farstey.

CONTINUED

GOT A POWERFUL SOFT SPOT FOR THE A-WING. I LEARNED TO FLY ON MY MOM'S RZ-1. IT HAS THE SMALLEST SILHOUETTE OF ANY REBELLION OR RESISTANCE FIGHTER AND TURNS FASTER THAN A SKYROCKET ON AN ICE SHEET. -POE

Lots of pilots tell the story about the time a single A-wing took out a Super Star Destroyer. But everybody disagrees about when and where it happened. -Poe

DOC #0532286-ALL

RZ-1 A-WING STARFIGHTER

Manufacturer: Kuat Systems Engineering

Length: 9.6 meters

Weapons: Two laser cannons, twelve concussion missiles

- Tight design plus dual engines equals speed and a small target profile.
- On maneuverability and sublight acceleration, the A-wing outclasses the TIE/IN interceptor.
- Hyperdrive does not require astromech for jump calculations.
- Sacrifices armor for speed; if factory-installed shield generator is removed, expect even greater performance boost at increased risk to pilot.

O&S can't condone procurement of additional A-wings at this time. In light of the disproportionate number of A-wings that Phoenix Squadron has lost to date. —Mothma

OFFICIAL REPORT

Colonel Bandwin Cor to General Dodonna

To answer the obvious question: yes, we should be using X-wings as the backbone of Starfighter Command. General Merrick agrees. Garven Dreis, the same. Unless you put a blaster to their head, neither will fly anything else.

Wise words! -Poe

They're both from Virujansi, so maybe it's because the X-wing handles like a bush hopper. It's something we're going to encounter more and more as we recruit from Rim worlds. Our hardware should match. Fortunately, the X-wing is the rare starfighter that can take on TIEs and Star Destroyers and everything in between.

Supplemental materials follow. Hopefully they'll persuade the accountants.

Having worked procurement and logistics, is it wrong to say that I sympathize with Grafis? Credits aren't infinite. Not everyone gets what they wish for. -Statura

I shall remember you said this, Statura. Admiral Ackbar

CONTINUED

THE NEW T-65 X-WING FIGHTER. TAKE WING.

Speed. Nimbleness. Firepower. Versatility.
An elegant 12.5 meters from nose to tail.
No craft can match it.

When you order, all these features are at your pilots' fingertips.

NOTE: THE ASTROMECH DROID SOCKET BEHIND COCKPIT FITS IA'S NEWEST MODELS.

1. Four Taim & Bak KX9 laser cannons
2. Two pairs of strike foils, which fold out for greater fire coverage
3. Two Krupx MG7 proton torpedo launchers, recessed into fuselage
4. Novaldex 04-Z cryogenic power generator
5. Chepat "Defender" deflector shield projector
6. Four 4L4 fusial thrust engines
7. Long-range hyperdrive
8. Carbanti transceiver sensor package
9. Transparisteel canopy

Compared to the Resistance's current T-70 X-wing squadrons, these stats still hold up pretty well. I'm always happy to fly a T-65.
-Poe

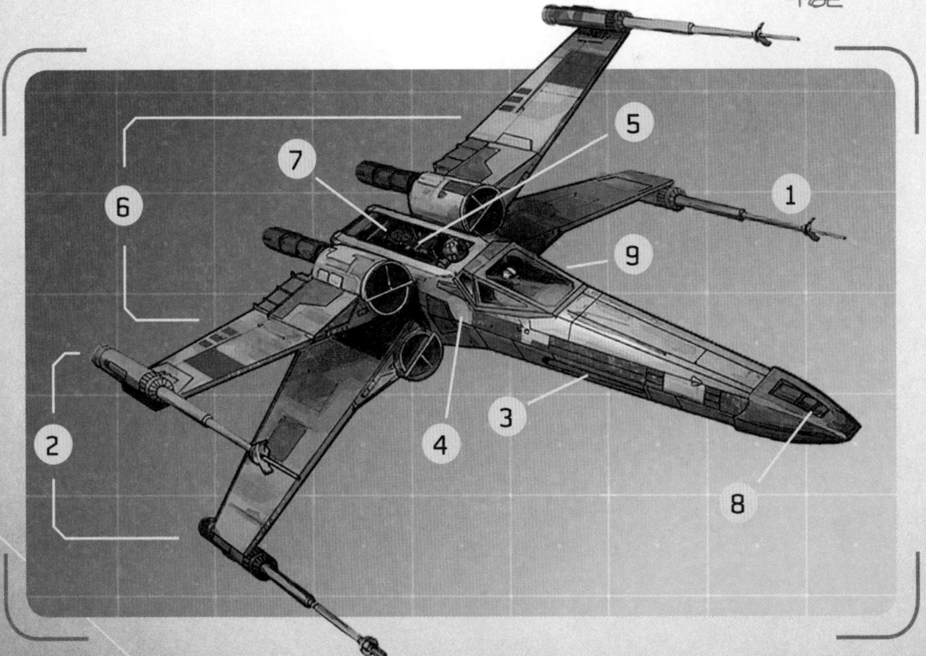

SHIP-TO-SHIP COMBAT

X-WING FLIGHT MANUAL

By Barion Raner (Blue Four)

Subsection Contents:

I MEMORIZED RANER'S RULES AS A KID! -POE

1. SPLIT S

Use the Split S to disengage from combat. After an inverted roll, dive vertically and pull out opposite to the enemy's vector.

Perform the maneuver when your attacker is closing from behind. A missile attack is typically made at a high closing speed. A laser attack will be made at a speed sufficient to pin you in the targeting reticle and minimize the enemy's chance of overshooting. The success of a Split S is dependent on the reaction speed of the X-wing's pilot.

MUST BE AN EARLY DRAFT. I REMEMBER THIS SECTION DIFFERENTLY. -POE

END DOCUMENT

MISSION #3920R

MISSION PLAN:

OPERATION BUCKLER

PLAN FILED BY:

GARVEN DREIS (RED LEADER)

OBJECTIVE:

Acquire decommissioned Y-wings from the orbital scrapyard at Ord Biniir

STRATEGY:

Employ subterfuge to avoid raising enemy suspicions concerning rebel mobilization in the Void of Chopani. A few X-wings have already found their way into pirate hands and are not uncommon in some Rim sectors. Our aim is to pose as pirates ourselves by emulating their appearance and flight tactics.

Several Red Squadron X-wings will need temporary pirate markings for this mission. See proposed designs.

KARÉ KUN WANTED TO DO SOMETHING LIKE THIS WHEN WE FLEW WITH RAPIER SQUADRON. WHY DID I DENY HER REQUEST? THESE LOOK INCREDIBLE!
-POE

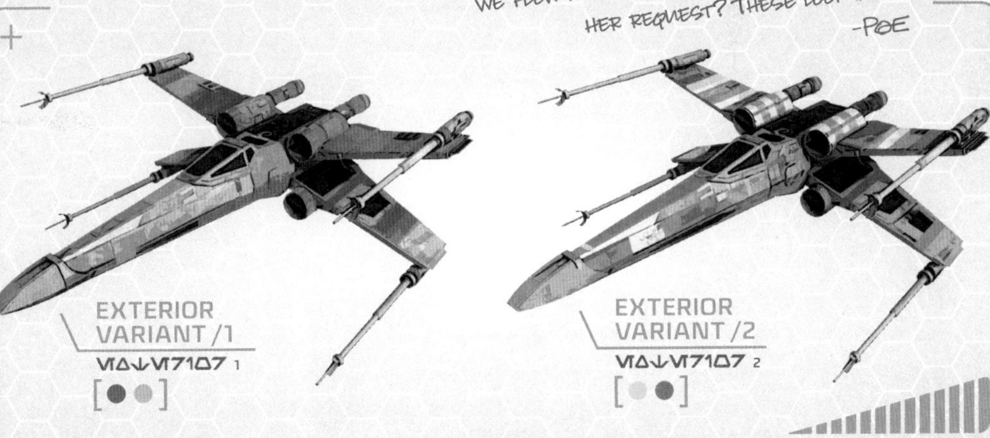

DOC #2535721-ALL

TO: GEN. DODONNA, SECTOR COMMAND

FROM: CMDR. SYNDULLA, PHOENIX LEADER

SUBJ: SHANTIPOLE MISSION

MISSION SUMMARY: Contact made with Mon Cal engineer Quarrie on Shantipole. With his blessing, I piloted his prototype fighter, the Blade Wing. The prototype's supercharged weapons proved sufficient to break the Imperial blockade of Ibaar. See secondary documentation for flight readouts.

Senator Organa is currently collaborating with Slayn & Korpil to manufacture additional B-wings. It may take some time before we see results. However, I believe the B-wing can replace the Y-wing as the Alliance's premier attack craft versus Imperial battleships.

A/SF-01 B-WING ASSAULT STARFIGHTER

THERE WASN'T A BETTER BOMBER ANYWHERE, AT LEAST NOT UNTIL THE RESISTANCE GOT ITS HANDS ON THE B/SF-17 HEAVY BOMBERS. STILL LOVE THESE SHIP SHREDDERS THOUGH. -POE

BASED ON B6 PROTOTYPE BLADE WING

MANUFACTURER: Slayn & Korpil
LENGTH: 16.9 meters

- Blockade buster/capital ship bomber—not optimized for dogfighting
- Constructed around a single airfoil
- Gyroscopic cockpit at one end remains level with horizon as airfoil spins around, weapons pod at other end, engine bank at center
- Laser cannons, proton torpedoes, ion cannons
- Two S-foils fold out to provide fire spread
- Integrated hyperdrive (no onboard astromech)

ACCORDING TO THE MECHANICS THIS THING IS A NIGHTMARE TO MAINTAIN. ON THE OTHER HAND THEY COMPLAIN ABOUT ALMOST EVERYTHING. -POE

NOTE: S&K engineers have rejected the following components of the Blade Wing prototype in the current production model:

- Composite-beam laser (drains energy from hyperdrive, risk of power surges)
- Second gunner's station (structurally unbalanced)

DATAFILES

DOC #4202820-ALL

TO: CMDR. MOTHMA

FROM: ADM. RADDUS

SUBJ: CURRENT FLEET STATUS

A clear-water assessment from Raddus. That didn't stop him from rushing into battle at Scarif.
—Admiral Ackbar

My aides Caitken and Shollan have assembled this on my behalf. Know this: we are scraping by on smaller vessels until we get the heavy hitters online. The Alliance is not yet ready for a fleet engagement against the Empire.

Our fleet, such as it is, largely consists of these ship classes:

DORNEAN GUNSHIP: We've lucked into a wealth of these Braha'tok-class gunships. Each is powerful given its size and can fit two starfighters on its undercarriage.

A gem among the smaller capital ships. Who still uses these?
-Statura

HAMMERHEAD CORVETTE: Powerful engines allowing it to work as a tug. Three dual laser cannons: two forward, one rear.

Dornea, my dear Statura. Dornea uses them.
—Admiral Ackbar

ALDERAANIAN CRUISER: Both the CR90 and CR70 corvettes are fast enough to serve as blockade runners. Most of our models have dual turbolaser turrets.

***PELTA*-CLASS FRIGATE:** A solid KDY design from the Clone Wars. We took these in as medcenter ships, but have since retrofitted a handful of them with turbolasers and point-defense lasers.

GALLOFREE TRANSPORTS: The GR-75 is the backbone of our fleet resupply efforts. Currently used as fuel tankers, fireships, medcenter ships, and troop transports. Twin laser turrets installed on most.

DOC #3552184-ALL

TO: CMDR. MOTHMA

FROM: COL. ANJ ZAVOR

SUBJ: UPDATE ON TELARIS SYSTEM OPERATIONS

The refugee Mon Cala city-ships in the Telaris cometary cloud have completed their conversion into war production facilities. The *Profundity* will be among the first combat-ready cruisers. Will supply ongoing updates as the launch date grows closer.

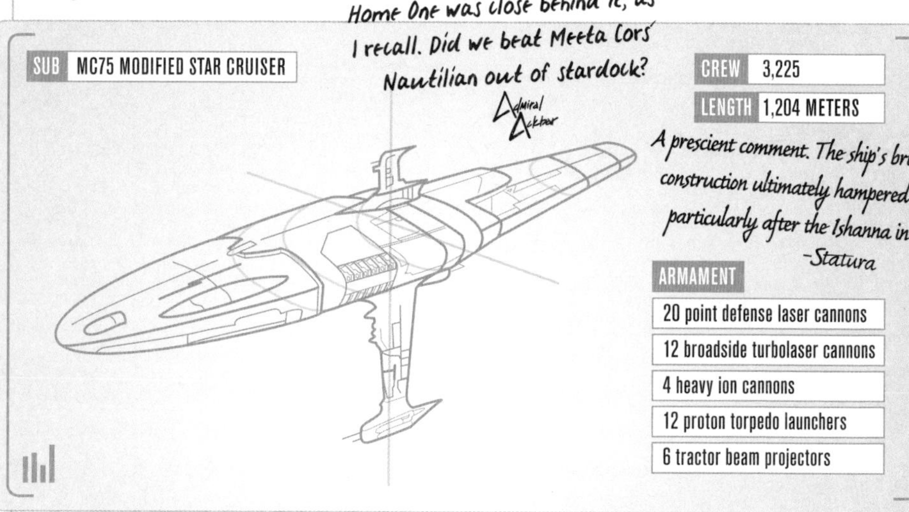

ADDENDUM:

We've acquired a *Quasar Fire*-class bulk cruiser in the Ryloth system, thanks to Commander Syndulla. If the Alliance can secure more of these ships, the Quasar Fire could fill the role of escort carrier.

A single Quasar Fire can accommodate up to forty-eight starfighters. According to a report issued by Mid-Rim Shipwrights, the structural integrity of its spaceframe is questionable, being subject to microfractures during realspace reversion.

TO: CMDR. MOTHMA

FROM: GEN. ONORAN, SPECFORCES

SUBJ: READINESS REPORT: SURFACE VEHICLES

Commander, please find below my assessment of the availability and relative strengths of the Alliance's ground vehicles, including assault tanks and armed hovercrafts. Additional insights have been provided by Lt. Sefla.

THE RESISTANCE IS ALARMINGLY UNDER EQUIPPED WHEN IT COMES TO GROUND VEHICLES. - EMATT

1. **Kelliak Freerunner**: Modular repulsorcraft with rotating gun platforms.

Sefla: Open-air cockpit limits environmental deployments. Great visibility until it starts raining.

2. **Mekuun Heavy Tracker**: Combat assault vehicle currently used as a mobile comm center. Omniprobe sensor array. Packs a long-range heavy laser cannon.

3. **ULAV (ultra-light assault vehicle)**: Small, fast repulsorcraft for a pilot and gunner. Two forward laser cannons and a rotating blaster cannon mounted on the rear, plus a concussion missile launcher.

4. **Aratech Arrow-23**: Combat-modified landspeeder. Laser cannon and concussion missile launcher. Can carry five troopers comfortably.

Sefla: Enclosed and armored, perfect for wilderness deployments. The weight of the armor can overtax the repulsor coils.

I'D GIVE ANYTHING TO HAVE A REPULSOR POOL ON D'QAR LOADED WITH ANY OF THESE MODELS, EVEN IF MOST OF THEM ARE OLDER THAN I AM. - EMATT

TALDOT SECTOR

Mon Mothma,

I have prepared the following report on the Empire's current level of military preparedness. I don't need to tell you that the Alliance is outmatched. Our situation is dire.

I have taken the liberty of scheduling a meeting for us to discuss these findings in person. Please come prepared to justify the Alliance's present course.

Sincerely,

Senator Vasp Vaspar

ALLIANCE MINISTER OF INDUSTRY

And today, when the New Republic controls the galaxy, our Resistance is outmatched by the hardware of the shrunken First Order. The Force must truly have faith in us, to always match us against such long odds. —Leia

DOC #3810126-ALL

TO: CMDR. MOTHMA

FROM: GEN. CRACKEN

SUBJ: IMPERIAL FLEET

Enclosed are the topline findings of agents operating in or near the following Imperial shipyards: Corellia, Kuat, Ringo Vinda, Allanteen VI, and Fondor.

STAR DESTROYERS

Star Destroyers are fast becoming the face of the Empire throughout the Rim. The smaller Venators, introduced during the Clone Wars, are still in production at Kuat Drive Yards. The Imperial Star Destroyer, however, is rapidly outpacing it as KD shipyards are converted to accommodate its scale.

1. Imperial Star Destroyer

LENGTH: 1,600 meters

ARMAMENT: Heavy turbolaser batteries, ion cannons, dual heavy turbolaser turrets, heavy ion cannon

Still in service, but supplanted on the front lines by the First Order's Resurgent-class battle cruiser. At 2,900 meters, it's nearly twice as long. -Statura

They say Snoke commands a flagship that dwarfs the old Super Star Destroyers. —Holdo

CONTINUED

turrets, quad heavy and medium turbolasers, tractor beam projectors. Carries TIE fighters and AT-ATs. Crew complement is nearly forty thousand.

2. Venator Star Destroyer
LENGTH: 1,137 meters
ARMAMENT: Heavy dual turbolaser turrets, medium dual turbolaser cannons, point-defense laser cannons, tractor beam projectors, heavy proton torpedo tubes. Carries starfighters, gunships, and walkers, as well as the modular components to erect a planetary garrison.

UPDATE: Imperial Interdictor
Full details still unknown. Cruiser equipped with four gravity well projectors—when powered, it can force ships out of hyperspace and prevent them from escaping. Prototype encountered and destroyed in Del Zennis system.

IMPERIAL PATROL CRAFT

Wherever possible, the Rebellion needs to pick fights it can win. This means Gozanti cruisers or smaller ships commonly deployed in Rim pickets and cargo inspections. X-wings or Y-wings can overwhelm one of these vessels and jump to safety before Imperial reinforcements arrive.

1. Gozanti cruiser
ARMAMENT: Twin laser turret, heavy laser cannon. Can carry four TIE starfighters (or two AT-ATs for ground deployment) by using exterior docking clamps.

2. Arquitens light cruiser
ARMAMENT: Quad laser turrets, dual turbolaser cannons, and missile tubes.

END DOCUMENT

DOC #3325345-ALL

TO: CMDR. MOTHMA
FROM: GEN. MERRICK
SUBJ: IMPERIAL STARFIGHTER CORPS

The TIE fighter's lack of shielding and dependence on a carrier for interstellar transport makes it comparatively weak versus most Alliance models. But that doesn't matter when the odds are 1:20 against us. Sienar Fleet Systems makes too many TIEs for us to handle, and as long as they keep finding bodies to fill the cockpits, we'll be the underdogs in starfighter superiority.

The standard TIE fighter is fast but flawed. No shields, no hyperdrive, and no life-support system reduces its mass for greater maneuverability. Has a pair of laser cannons mounted at the base of the cockpit.

WE'D BE SCORING A LOT MORE KILLS IF THIS WERE STILL THE CASE. THAT MEANS FIRST ORDER PILOTS AREN'T BEING TREATED LIKE THROWAWAYS, AND I'VE GOT TO ADMIT THAT'S A GOOD THING. -POE

The Sienar engineers aren't sitting still. They're committed to the solar panel/ion engine system, and continue to find countless ways to reexpress that basic equation. As with all things Imperial, these listings are far from complete

1. **TIE/sa bomber**: Two distinctive, elongated spaceframe pods—one houses the pilot, the other the payload. In addition to whatever detonite it's dropping, the TIE bomber has homing missiles and a pair of laser cannons.

2. **TIE/IN interceptor**: This is the design I'm most worried about. Dagger-shaped solar arrays feed an advanced ion-stream projector. It's incredibly agile. Only our A-wings are capable of matching it in dogfights.

3. **TIE striker**: It's experimental, but the TIE/sk x1 air superiority fighter is a demon in atmospheric environments. Comes with four laser cannons and two heavy laser cannons, and some models have a bomb chute.

4. **TIE reaper**: This one's a troop carrier, not a starfighter, but it wears all the hallmarks of TIE design. The reaper is only armed with two laser cannons but its shields and its tough spaceframe can absorb punishment long

CONTINUED

enough for it to unload troopers—usually elite Death Troopers, so that's another thing to watch out for.

5. TIE Advanced v1: The Empire's Inquisitors appear to have first dibs on these prototypes. Unusual for TIEs, the v1s have shields, hyperdrives, and folding wing panels. They're armed with dual laser cannons and warheads. One of these fell into our hands after the action at Mustafar and Harinar's crew has had a merry time taking it apart.

6. TIE Advanced x1: Our current assessment is that this is the next generation of the v1. Angled solar arrays, two heavy laser cannons, a missile launcher, a shield generator, and a hyperdrive. We don't have much to go on yet, other than the Phoenix recordings that demonstrate how effortlessly a single Advanced x1 carved through an entire rebel squadron.

7. TIE defender: We don't know what to make of these. A unique configuration to say the least. It's a shielded, hyperspace-capable starfighter with three angled solar panels and two laser cannons on each wing. Also packs warhead launchers and a tractor beam projector. In my opinion, these will probably remain rare.

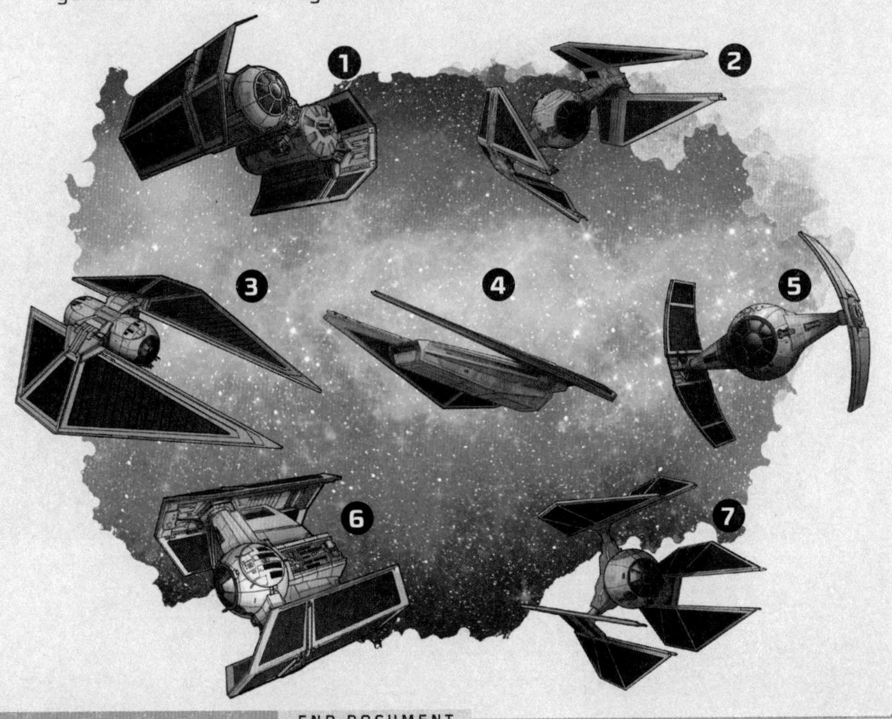

END DOCUMENT

DOC #3491295-ALL

TO: CMDR. MOTHMA

FROM: GEN. ONORAN

SUBJ: IMPERIAL GROUND ASSAULT

"Combined arms" underlies the Empire's approach to surface warfare, integrating multiple military types from infantry to armor. This strategy too often hits the Alliance where it is weakest by forcing us to defend against one type of attack and leaving us vulnerable to another.

These vehicles—when deployed alongside stormtroopers—bring the full power of Imperial combined arms to bear.

1. All Terrain Armored Transport (AT-AT): Troop transport with two heavy laser cannons on the chin and two variable-elevation medium repeating blasters on either side of the head. It can carry up to forty stormtroopers. One common variant, the AT-ACT, has fewer guns and a removable cargo section built into its body.

2. All Terrain Scout Transport (AT-ST): The scout walker is lightly armored and commonly used in urban patrols. Armed with a double blaster cannon, a single blaster cannon, and a concussion grenade launcher.

3. All Terrain Defense Pod (AT-DP): Police patrols on Rim worlds often incorporate AT-DPs. Has a heavily armored head and a single laser cannon on its chin.

THE FIRST ORDER'S ALL TERRAIN PATROL DROID, OR AT-PD, IS A FULLY-AUTOMATED CRAWLER ARMED WITH TWO HEAVY LASER CANNONS. I HOPE TO HAVE SOME ARMORED VEHICLES OF MY OWN WHEN I FINALLY FACE THEM. - EMATT

4. "Occupier" combat assault tank: Another vehicle often assigned to urban duty. Armed with two elevating double laser cannons and one medium double laser cannon, and is frequently accompanied by marching infantry. Comes in both repulsorlift and treaded models.

5. HAVw A6 Juggernaut: A heavy-assault vehicle left over from the Clone Wars and every bit as dangerous as an AT-AT. Absolutely gigantic—carrying up to three hundred troopers—and armed with a turret-mounted heavy laser cannon, a rapid repeating laser cannon, four antipersonnel cannons, and two concussion missile launchers. The Juggernaut also has a little brother, the scaled-down HCVw A9 turbo tank.

Request understood, Major. I sympathize. It's not as if we have them locked away in a vault. —Leia

CONTINUED

6. Imperial-class 1-H repulsortank: Found more frequently in the Mid Rim and places coreward. Sports a heavy laser cannon, a medium blaster cannon, and two blaster cannons mounted on the sides. According to Imperial chatter, it is prone to breaking down in bad weather.

7. Imperial troop transport: Common on occupied planets and pretty much invisible everywhere else. Armed with two forward-mounted laser cannons and a twin blaster turret. Easily identified by its six open-air passenger pockets, three to a side.

END DOCUMENT

Mon Mothma—please review and provide your approval for distribution. As discussed, we have expurgated all mentions of Saw Gerrera's Partisans.—Gen. Onoran

COMBAT TACTICS

REBEL FIELD MANUAL

By Sergeant Ruescott Melshi, Alliance SpecForces

Marines, pathfinders, urban guerrillas, techs, wilderness fighters, heavy weapons specialists, and infiltrators make up Special Forces. We infiltrate. We exfiltrate. We go in first and strike from cover. We do this better than the Empire, and that is how we'll win this war.

Melshi. Gone too soon, but it's good to see the old Nek name once more. I served with him on Gaulus. – Ematt

SUBSECTION CONTENTS:

1. Stormtroopers: Class Identification
2. Guerrilla Tactics
3. Planetary Drop Zones

1. STORMTROOPERS: CLASS IDENTIFICATION

The Empire now relies on recruits to fill its ranks, but the Stormtrooper Corps isn't really all that different than the clone trooper army of the late Republic.

Each stormtrooper wears an eighteen-piece armor set made of white plastoid. Weak points in the armor include the gap between the chest plate and the shoulder armor. Stormtroopers also have notoriously poor peripheral vision.

A. **Tank troopers**: Trained for recon and skirmishes, and usually attached to ground assault vehicles like the Occupier. If you can catch them outside of their tanks, their light armor doesn't offer much protection.

B. **Magmatroopers**: The Empire's domination of the galaxy's mining worlds has made the magmatrooper a necessity. Their variant armor can withstand extremes of up to 1,900 degrees.

C. **Sandtroopers**: Typically stationed on hot, dry worlds of sand or ash. Armor incorporates breathing filters and cooling recirculators.

D. **Scout troopers**: Specialists in mobile reconnaissance, biker scouts pilot 74-Z speeder bikes and wear lightweight, nonrestrictive armor.

E. **Snowtroopers**: Cold-assault stormtroopers have a distinctive breather hood covering their helmet faceplate used to recirculate warm air. They are often trained as survivalists.

F. Shoretroopers: Fairly uncommon, the coastal defender stormtrooper is optimized for tropical environments. Wears lightweight, sand-colored armor. Squad leaders wear a kama attached to their belt.

G. Rocket troopers: Also called jump troopers, these soldiers don't handle their jet packs nearly as well as the Mandalorians. But they will jump to high ground to launch air-to-ground attacks on entrenched positions.

H. Death troopers: Extremely rare, these are elite soldiers who serve Imperial Intelligence as bodyguards and special-missions experts. Their black armor is coated in a material that warps electronic signals, allowing them to hide from sensor sweeps.

Small blessing that she didn't have to deal with the cyborg killers of the Guavian Death Gang or the ex-Hutt retainers now operating as Kanjiklub. Since the Empire's fall, the underworld has risen.
—Leia

MOTHMA | JOURNAL ENTRY

I DON'T LIKE DEALING WITH CRIMINALS. THE HUTTS ARE VENAL OPPORTUNISTS. BLACK SUN MEMBERS ARE SLAVERS AND ASSASSINS. THE CRYMORAH AND THE DROID GOTRA TURN MY STOMACH.

BUT I AM NOT DEAF TO THE CONCERNS OF THOSE URGING ME TO COMPROMISE, TO PURSUE LESS RIGOROUS SOLUTIONS IN THE SHORT TERM. TO BEND, LEST THE ALLIANCE BREAK.

I HAVE ALLOWED GENERAL DRAVEN TO SEND ONE OF HIS BEST, CAPTAIN ANDOR, TO REOPEN DISCUSSIONS WITH THE HUTT COUNCIL. FOR THE TIME BEING, WE WILL USE OUR EMBEDDED SPIES TO KEEP TABS ON THE OTHER CRIMINAL FACTIONS.

CLASSIFIED DOCUMENT—CLEARANCE LEVEL:

ANDOR/DRAVEN PROG31052

RI 311-B6

BHG

TO: GENERAL DRAVEN

FROM: CAPTAIN ANDOR

Our agent in the Bounty Hunters Guild reports that sentiment is trending negative toward the Rebellion as the Empire increases its use of guild services.

In other words, Cradossk is making a killing. Moffs with deep pockets are willing to pay big for bounty hunters who can make their problems disappear. The Imperial Office of Criminal Investigation has a whole arm dedicated to working with the BHG.

Will they still take our money? Of course. But on jobs of any real consequence, we're going to get outbid by the Empire.

AGREED, WITH RESERVATIONS. FORTUNATELY THE FIRST ORDER DOESN'T SEEM TO WANT TO DO BUSINESS WITH THE GUILD, POSSIBLY FOR IDEOLOGICAL REASONS.
- EMATT

The guild isn't what it used to be, and because of that there could be no better time for the Resistance to forge a partnership.
-Holdo

DOC #2250135-ALL

TO: CMDR. MOTHMA
FROM: GEN. DRAVEN
SUBJ: MINING GUILD

Disappointing news from the Hutt Council and the Bounty Hunters Guild, I know. Let me advance another possibility: the Mining Guild.

The guild operates under the blessing of the Empire, but its roots are far older than Palpatine. Theirs is a marriage of convenience, not ideology. I believe the Alliance can secure concessions of safe passage from the Mining Guild, and the cost might be less than you think.

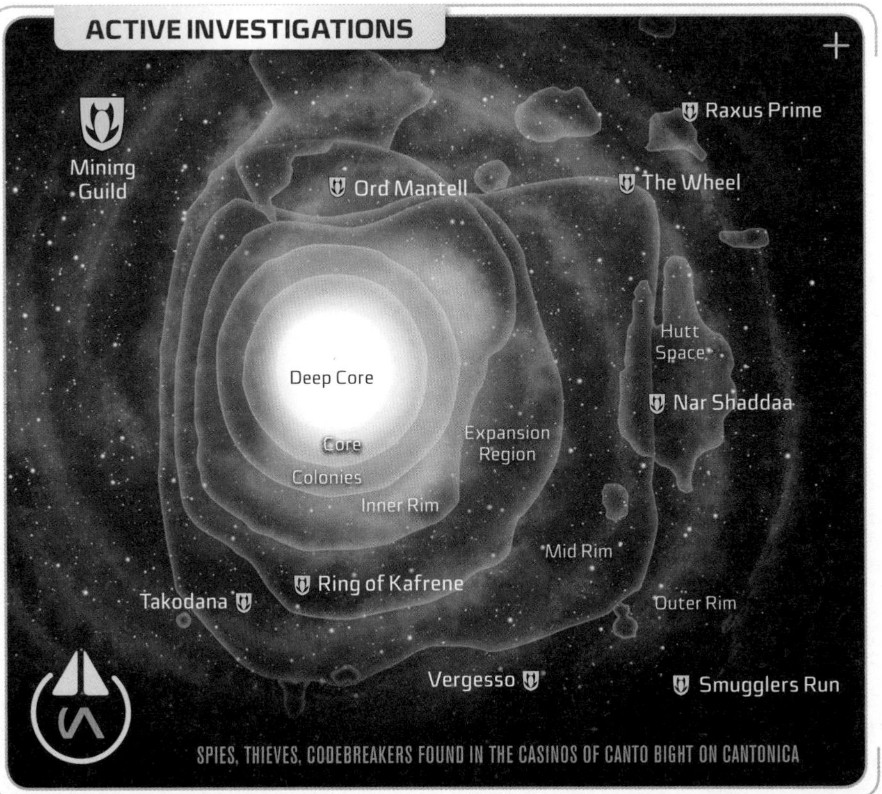

ACTIVE INVESTIGATIONS

Mining Guild
Raxus Prime
Ord Mantell
The Wheel
Hutt Space
Deep Core
Nar Shaddaa
Core
Expansion Region
Colonies
Inner Rim
Mid Rim
Ring of Kafrene
Takodana
Outer Rim
Vergesso
Smugglers Run

SPIES, THIEVES, CODEBREAKERS FOUND IN THE CASINOS OF CANTO BIGHT ON CANTONICA

Dantooine
Generis
Mantooine
Fest
Reegian system
INSET
Ralltiir
Chandrila
Alderaan
Kashyyyk
New Plympto
DEEP CORE
CORE
COLONIES
INNER RIM
MID RIM
Tomark
Edan II
EXPANSION REGION
Golrath
OUTER RIM
Sullust
D'Qar
Vergesso
Isis
Polis Massa

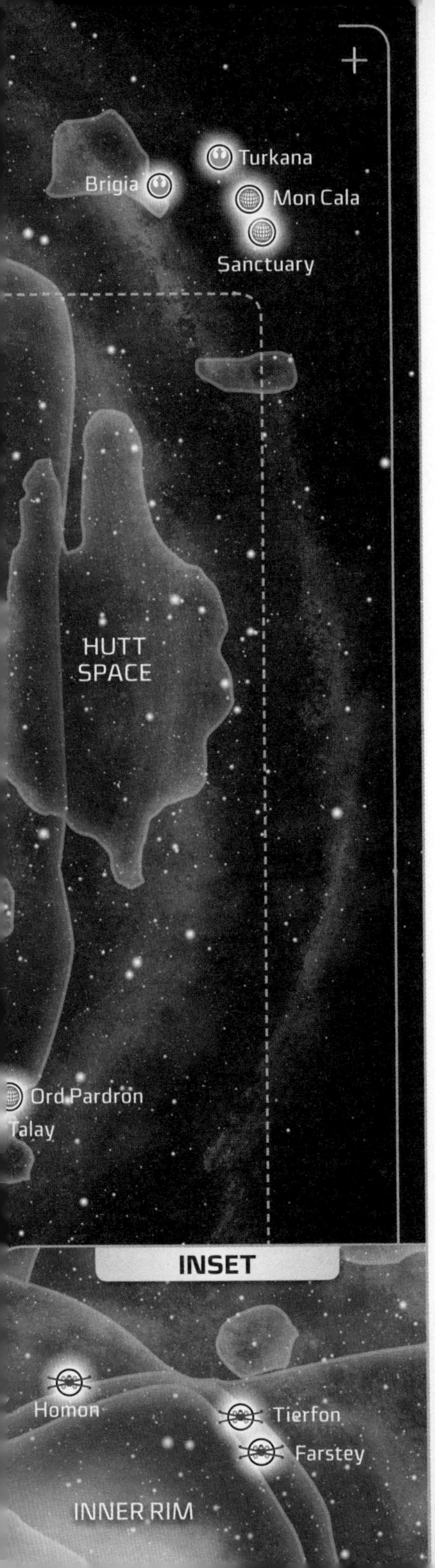

Turkana
Brigia
Mon Cala
Sanctuary
HUTT SPACE
Ord Pardron
Talay

INSET

Homon
Tierfon
Farstey
INNER RIM

LEGEND

REBEL OPERATIONS SECTOR/REGIONAL HQS

- Talay
- Golrath
- Vergesso
- Polis Massa
- Tomark
- Brigia
- Turkana
- Mantooine/Fest
- Generis
- Edan II
- Dantooine

STARFIGHTER HUBS LEVEL 5 OR HIGHER

- Tierfon
- Homon
- Farstey

PLANETARY ALLIES ALLIANCE SAFE WORLDS

- Alderaan
- Ralltiir
- Sanctuary
- Kashyyyk
- New Plympto
- Sullust
- Ord Pardron
- Chandrila
- Isis
- Mon Cala

SHADOW PLANETS DEEP SPACE CACHES

- D'Qar
- Reegian system

Didn't we build up D'Qar during this era? Or was that later?
—Leia

IT WAS LATER, POST-YAVIN. MIRRIN PRIME TOO. I SHOULD KNOW; MY SHRIKES SCOUTED THEM BOTH.
- EMATT

ENCODED LAYER (OUTER RIM):
INPUT BREAKER KEY //7567 TO DISPLAY
Republic bases, Separatist installations, pirate hideouts, smugglers dens, Mandalorian outposts

DOC #2440135-ALL

TO: GEN. DODONNA, SECTOR COMMAND

FROM: LT. HEFF TOBBER, BLUE SQUADRON

SUBJ: CRAIT BASE

Ackbar, Statura, Holdo—take note. —Leia

General, as you know I assisted in the evacuation of Crait base. Though we abandoned it in a hurry, we left most of its facilities intact in the hope of returning at a later date with heavy transport equipment.

The comm center is still functional (though locked down and powered off). There's still a squadron of skim speeders in the hangar.

I'm not worried about scavengers. The system's coordinates aren't on any chart, and even if the old mining company left its logs somewhere, the base itself is a vault. Fusioncutters won't take a chip out of that durasteel gate, and the rest of the base sits in the heart of a mountain.

I said as much at the time: diffusion and mobility are th[e] keys to survival. Most didn['t] come around to m[y] way of think[ing] until afte[r] Hoth. Admiral Ackbar

MON MOTHMA TO GENERAL DODONNA

General, concerning the Alliance's use of a central HQ for command staff, you have my provisional support. Dantooine will continue to serve as the meeting hub for executive-level discussions.

However, I do not wish to sacrifice our mobility. Admiral Raddus will keep our fleet on the move, and sensitive assets will be kept in the direct possession of agents whom I know and trust.

MON MOTHMA TO BAIL ORGANA

I feel I can take no other action.

I know you have worked with Gerrera as recently as the mission to Geonosis. But he has grown crueler and harder, and the brutality of the Partisans is actively harming our cause.

MON MOTHMA TO BAIL ORGANA

That sort of extremism is what allows the Empire to paint us all as extremists. Planetary governments that might otherwise be sympathetic to our plight now refuse to meet with our delegates. They believe the worst about Saw, and they assume I condone his crimes. And why wouldn't they? When have we ever taken a stand against our own?

I will be issuing a motion to formally censure Saw Gerrera and cut him off from any contact with our forces. Our Rebel Alliance will not include Gerrera or his Partisans.

RESOLUTION OF CENSURE CONDEMNING SAW GERRERA OF THE PARTISANS

In his conduct as a resistance leader and a member of the Alliance to Restore the Republic, Saw Gerrera, in violation of his vows to honor the Alliance's standards governing humane behavior including the traditions established under the Ruusan Armistice, has acted in a fashion contrary to the laws of civilized behavior and engaged in acts of moral repugnance unjustified under a state of war.

Saw Gerrera's Partisans, under Gerrera's sole leadership and direction, have targeted civilians and innocents, have employed cruel methods of interrogation, and have refused to respond to repeated concerns raised by Alliance representatives. It is concluded that Saw Gerrera has not acted in a fashion worthy of the Alliance's respect and trust.

It is hereby resolved, by the Chief of State of the Alliance to Restore the Republic and the members of the Alliance Council, that Saw Gerrera be condemned for acting in a manner incompatible with the laws and ideals of this body.

OFFICIAL DOC: #Z1252K-22

ꓥ NOTICE |||| BY IMPERIAL DECREE ALL CITIZENS MUST SUBMIT ANY INFORMATION REGARDING REBEL INSURGENTS

WANTED

FOR CRIMES AGAINST THE EMPIRE

WANTED: Saw Gerrera • Male Insurgent Traitor
SHOULD BE CONSIDERED ARMED AND DANGEROUS. USE CAUTION.

HEIGHT: 1.87m GENDER: Male RACE: Human AGE: Unknown

The Empire is seeking the capture, or positive proof of death, of known rebel leader

KNOWN ASSOCIATES: Beezer Fortuna, Moroff, Weeteef Cyu-Bee, Tognath eggmates Benthic "Two Tubes" and Edrio "Two Tubes"

It is the will of Emperor Palpatine to ensure the future of a stable and prosperous galaxy

TRINEBULON NEWS

The Truth, Straight from the Source

SENATOR MOTHMA STEPS DOWN

Imperial Center, Coruscant—A shocking development today in the Imperial Senate, as Senator Mon Mothma of Chandrila denounced Emperor Palpatine before the assembled legislature.

"I name the Emperor himself for ordering the brutal attacks on the people of Ghorman," Mon Mothma stated. "Their peaceful world is one of countless systems helpless against his oppressive rule. This massacre is proof that our self-appointed 'Emperor' is little more than a lying executioner, imposing his tyranny on the pretense of security. We cannot allow this evil to stand."

Reaction in the Senate chamber was swift and near unanimous. Loyal senators condemned the remarks with angry shouts that drowned out scattered pockets of applause. The embattled senator withdrew with her aides and refused to address her critics. A representative told *TriNebulon News* that Mon Mothma could not be reached for comment.

This is when she stopped living a double life. My father and I would have followed in due time, even if the Emperor hadn't disbanded the Senate.

—Leia

ISB agents came to Cantham House to question us. They knew we knew something. They just couldn't prove it. —Leia

ERT · ALERT · ALERT · ALERT · ALER

IMPERIAL SECURITY BUREAU ALERT

IMPERIAL SENATOR MON MOTHMA HAS FLED CORUSCANT FOLLOWING HER TREASONOUS REMARKS AGAINST HIS IMPERIAL MAJESTY.

ALL CITIZENS ARE URGED TO REMAIN VIGILANT AND IMMEDIATELY REPORT ANY INFORMATION THAT COULD LEAD TO HER CAPTURE.

FURTHER ISB UPDATES TO COME.

DOC #2782357-ALL

TO: GEN. DODONNA, SECTOR COMMAND
FROM: CAPT. VANDER, GOLD LEADER
SUBJ: POST-MISSION REPORT: OPERATION HANDOFF

Gold Squadron's Y-wings escorted the transport carrying Sen. Mon Mothma and her attaché Erskin Semaj to Dantooine. At a fueling stop, an Imperial patrol attacked. Gold Squadron engaged the enemy.

The transport sustained critical damage, Mon Mothma and her aide evacuated to the freighter *Ghost*. After beating back the Imperials, Gold Squadron and the *Ghost* jumped to hyperspace.

HENDRI UNDERHOLT

Senator! I can't believe what just happened! Erskin offered to get me offworld.

MON MOTHMA

I'm glad to hear it. I wanted to ask you myself but it wouldn't have been fair. This is dangerous. By following me you're committing treason.

HENDRI UNDERHOLT

I would never abandon you, especially not now, when you need friends more than ever.

MON MOTHMA

I'll see you soon, Hendri. It's a new experience, being on the run.

MOTHMA | JOURNAL ENTRY

TIES HAVE BEEN CUT. PLANS ARE IN MOTION. BY RESIGNING FROM THE SENATE, I CAN MORE EFFECTIVELY LEAD THIS REBEL ALLIANCE, BUT THE EMPEROR'S WRATH WILL BE TERRIBLE.

THINGS ARE GOING TO GET WORSE BEFORE THEY GET BETTER, AND SPLINTERING INTO FACTIONS MAY YET BE THE ALLIANCE'S UNDOING. THEREFORE, I AM TAKING PREEMPTIVE STEPS TO ENCOURAGE COOPERATION.

AS HEAD OF HIGH COMMAND, I WILL INCORPORATE INSIGHTS FROM BOTH THE POLITICAL AND PARAMILITARY SIDES OF THE REBELLION. OLD SOLDIERS LIKE RADDUS CAN'T IMAGINE ANY SOLUTION THAT DOESN'T INVOLVE FIGHTING. IDEALISTS LIKE PAMLO IMAGINE A NEGOTIATED PEACE IN WHICH PALPATINE RELINQUISHES CONTROL TO THE SENATE.

THESE INDIVIDUALS WILL MAKE UP THE REBEL COUNCIL. I KNOW THEM WELL, WHICH IS WHY I KNOW THAT PUTTING THEM IN THE SAME ROOM WILL BE . . . MESSY.

I didn't believe this myself, but I thought the Senate could still achieve something. For years, we moved pieces from one square to another, unaware that our opponent had long since abandoned the game.

—Leia

Gen. Jan Dodonna
Sector Command

Col. Bandwin Cor
Starfighter Command

Adm. Raddus
Fleet Command
(liaison: Col. Anj Zavor)

Gen. Pitt Onoran
Special Forces

Gen. Davits Draven
Alliance Intelligence

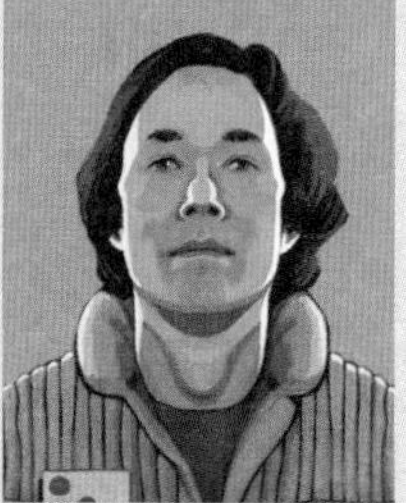

Col. Haxen Delto
Alliance Intelligence
(communications)

Maj. Capin Harinar
Alliance Intelligence
(technology)

Gen. Baccam Grafis
Ordnance & Supply

Gen. Dustil Forell
Support Services

Sen. Bail Organa (Alderaan)
Secretary of the Cabinet

Sen. Nower Jebel (Uyter)
Minister of Finance

Sen. Vasp Vaspar (Taldot)
Minister of Industry

Sen. Tynnra Pamlo (Taris)
Minister of Education

DOC #2788889-ALL

TO: REBEL COUNCIL

FROM: MON MOTHMA

SUBJ: DECLARATION OF THE REBEL ALLIANCE

Following is the address I will make within the hour. It will go out across all Alliance comm channels and will be inserted into the public holonet wherever we have a satellite splice. Trillions of beings will soon hear my voice. This is a galaxy-wide call to arms. We can no longer fight in isolation. Today is the first day of the Rebel Alliance. Together, we will restore the Republic.

This is Senator Mon Mothma. I've been called a traitor for speaking out against a corrupt Galactic Senate, a Senate manipulated by the sinister tactics of the Emperor. For too long, I've watched the heavy hand of the Empire strangle our liberties, stifling our freedoms in the name of ensuring our safety. No longer.

Despite Imperial threats, despite the Emperor himself, I have no fear as I take new action. For I am not alone. Beginning today, we stand together as allies.

I hereby resign from the Senate to fight for you. Not from the distant halls of politics but from the front lines.

We will not rest until we bring an end to the Empire, until we restore the Republic. Are you with me?

SHELL TOP-LEVEL/CATEGORY

ALLIANCE CHRON 2

ABSTRACT:
Organizing the Rebellion

Hendri Underholt

ARCHIVIST

STANDARD DATE: 14–17 AFE

(AFTER THE FORMATION OF THE EMPIRE)

An ultimate weapon? It doesn't exist. It can never exist.

Nothing short of complete extermination could ever snuff the flames of resistance. No scouring could ever be that thorough.

Saw would disagree. I remember the meetings, the long shuttle rides, Saw holding forth on the Empire's fixation with symbols of power. In his view, unchecked egomania always ends in genocide.

If only I still possessed such optimism. Admiral Ackbar

I reject that calculus. I reject it firmly and with a well-considered conscience. It is hardly the only thing on which Saw and I disagree, but I refuse to humor such monumental cynicism. Palpatine was once Naboo's senator. Palpatine was once a <u>boy</u>. No one can live among others for so long and ultimately abandon any attempt at cooperation and coexistence.

People are capable of great evil, it's true. But even they are capable of redemption. —Leia

If the rumors of the Tarkin Initiative are true and the Empire is indeed developing what they consider an "ultimate weapon," it can only be a deterrent. To use it would be monstrous and counterproductive. No one wishes death on an indiscriminate scale, not with the Clone Wars so fresh in our collective memories.

I believe there is goodness in all things, even in my enemies. It's what keeps me from falling to cynicism and ending up like Saw.

RI 395-X1

INTEL SUMMARY CIC

TO: COMMANDER MOTHMA

FROM: GENERAL CRACKEN

As requested, this doc contains a high-level overview of possible Imperial superweapon projects, including theoretical work that Senator Vaspar would call "spacer's tales." However, I feel these rumors provide directional insight concerning the Empire's habit of seeking cataclysmic solutions to every problem.

You know Colonel Delto; he's our best source for eavesdropping on Imperial chatter. Don't know if you've spent much time with Major Harinar outside of council briefings, but he has a knack for reverse engineering captured tech.

TO: Cracken

FROM: Harinar

RE: Your weapons request

NOTE: RUN ALL THIS BY RESISTANCE INTEL. SOME OF THESE ARE ALREADY IN THE HISTORY LOGS, BUT OTHERS COULD HAVE BEEN RESTARTED UNDER THE FIRST ORDER. - EMATT

1. ELECTRO-PROTON BOMB/DEFOLIATOR

These are two halves of the same chip! The Republic used the EPB during the Clone Wars to devastate electronics within a blast radius while leaving organic troopers unharmed. The Separatist defoliator did the opposite, shredding organic molecular bonds to leave lifeless metal behind. Combining them? It's child's play. Note the Empire has a number of ex-Sep researchers working for Krennic (see doc 41.2647).

2. MEGA-ION CANNON

The Clone Wars version of this tech was built into the Separatist flagship *Malevolence* (a *Subjugator*-class) but it was destroyed in the Prindaar system. Layered resonators build up an ion charge until it can wreck a small fleet. Haven't seen this in the Empire's armada and I'm not sure why.

CONTINUED

CRACKEN/MOTHMA PROG38808

3. BLUE SHADOW VIRUS

I'm no pathologist, but biological agents remain an urgent threat. The Blue Shadow Virus kills carbon-based life-forms with a 96 percent success rate and has been weaponized repeatedly during wartime. We are woefully ill prepared to guard against a targeted pandemic.

TO: Cracken

FROM: Delto

RE: IMP weapons projects

1. TORPEDO SPHERE

Transmitter traffic from Loronar is spiking. We're going to be looking at a whole constellation of battlemoons if the Empire can pump these out. These two-kilometer siege platforms are armed with hundreds of proton torpedo tubes that can crack any planetary shield, given time and patience. I've been monitoring equipment suppliers, and I'm telling you we should be worried.

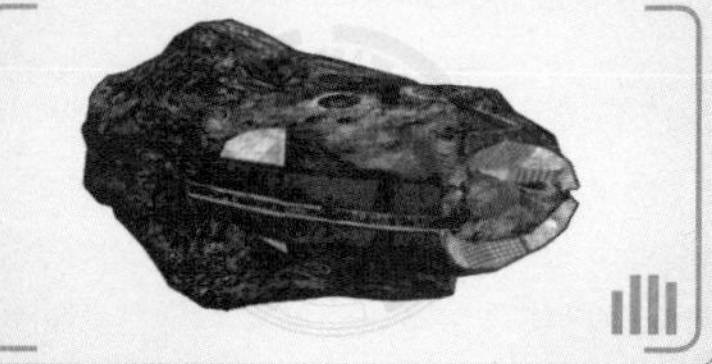

2. ASTEROID DREADNOUGHT

Stories have emerged of a supership disguised as a space rock. I'm not going to throw them out, but I must emphasize that our source inside Patriim is unreliable.

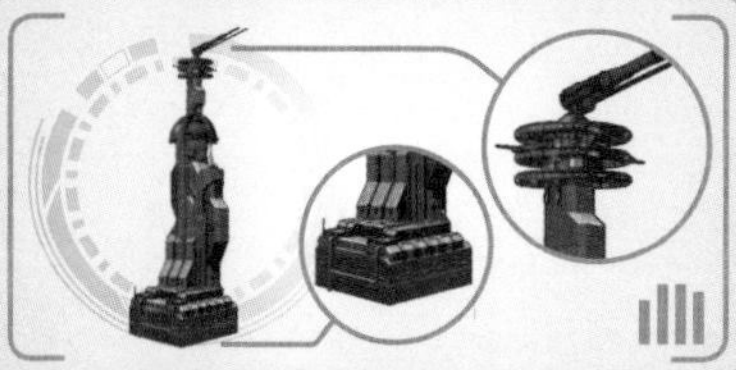

3. OMEGA FROST

The infamous interstellar freeze ray is, in my expert opinion, General, intentional disinformation.

4. MASS SHADOW GENERATOR

One of history's tall tales? Maybe. But a generator capable of existing in hyperspace and realspace simultaneously would be bad news. Fortunately, nothing suggests the Empire has made any breakthroughs.

END DOCUMENT

MON MOTHMA TO AIREN CRACKEN

We chatted about this over last night's ales. I know you don't have all the answers. But I need your best estimate on the nature and scope of the Tarkin Initiative. I know Tarkin. He's a heartless skeleton held together by the stiffness of his uniform. Airen, what is this ghoul up to?

Oh, well said. —Leia

CLASSIFIED DOCUMENT—CLEARANCE LEVEL: 

CRACKEN/MOTHMA PROG300653

TARKIN INITIATIVE

TO: CMDR. MOTHMA

FROM: GEN. CRACKEN

You know it physically pains me to deliver speculation. This is the worst thing you could have asked me to do, worse even than when you dared me to finish that glass of kri'gee.

Let me start with the Tarkin Doctrine, which as you know is a political philosophy with three platforms: territorial consolidation, centralized control of information, and a governing style based on fear. The Tarkin Initiative seems to be how Wilhuff Tarkin plans to back up that third point.

THEY GOT THEIR HANDS ON A BOTTLE OF KRI'GEE? I WAS BORN FIFTY YEARS TOO LATE. -POE

It's not enough that he can summon the galaxy's star fleet with one call to the Emperor. He craves consolidated power, under his control. Hence the Tarkin Initiative, a think tank within the Advanced Weapons Research division. There's a lot going on under that canopy. Too much to sum up here.

KEY POINTS:

- Tarkin isn't running his initiative day to day. It falls under Orson Krennic (will resend dossier).
- Project Celestial Power (see RI-X3871) is part of the Tarkin Initiative. Maybe it's a free-energy breakthrough? Senator Vaspar thinks so, but I disagree. Anything that touches Tarkin is poison. If Celestial Power is feasible, Tarkin could use that energy to fuel a superweapon.

The Tarkin Doctrine still holds sway in the First Order, if their habit of building ever-larger warships is anything to go by. -Holdo

DOC #27798689-ALL

TO: CMDR. MOTHMA

FROM: GEN. CRACKEN

SUBJ: IMPERIAL DIRECTOR ORSON KRENNIC

Orson Krennic: Currently director of Advanced Weapons Research for the Tarkin Initiative within the Imperial Security Bureau. 51 standard years old; born on Lexrul, Sativran City. Notably, Krennic has no connections within the Empire's most prominent political or naval families.

For playing such a significant role in Imperial weapons development, Krennic received little credit in historical annals. That would have irritated him, and for that I'm glad. —Leia

Background:

- Identified as a prodigy at an early age
- Studied architecture at the Brentaal Futures Program
- During the Clone Wars, oversaw the repurposing of Coruscant municipal spaces into military command centers
- Held postwar administrative post at Coruscant's Institute of Applied Science, where he screened scientists for expertise in energy manipulation, materials science, and theoretical physics
- Became director for Project Celestial Power during the early years of the Empire

(continued on p. 2)

GEN. DRAVEN TO MON MOTHMA

You see what I have to deal with. But it is information, nonetheless. Weems is talented but unaccustomed to the military command structure. Expect more follow-up on this subject should Intelligence deem it worthy.

CONTINUED

GEN. DRAVEN TO MON MOTHMA

TO: GEN. DRAVEN, ALLIANCE INTELLIGENCE
FROM: PVT. WEEMS, SIGNALS INTEL TECH
SUBJ: WHAT ARE THESE?!

Sir, I know you told me to relax after today's shift, but I took the intercept packet back to my quarters and ran all of my threaded dataslicers on the encrypted algorithm. I thought they wouldn't be done until morning, but I already got something!

It's only headers. The deep copy is behind another layer still, and I think it might actually be unrecoverable no matter what we do because of the hyperstorms that were going on when we cut this packet out of the Balmorra relay. But sir! The headers!

- Stellarsphere
- Pax Aurora
- Black Saber
- War Mantle
- Ion Ring
- Cluster Prism

What are these? Imperial counterintelligence campaigns? Code names for upcoming military strikes? Classified weapons projects?

I know it's not much to go on but thanks for taking a look. Have a good night!!

Interesting, I never saw this report at the time. Should we have been more vigilant in pursuing these leads?
—Leia

END

CLASSIFIED DOCUMENT—CLEARANCE LEVEL: 

DRAVEN/CRACKEN PROG38906

RI 467-X1
INTEL SUMMARY CIC
TO: GENERAL CRACKEN
FROM: GENERAL DRAVEN

You've already seen the reports, so I'm going to focus on their legitimacy. This is real, Airen. I can't vouch for the defector himself, but this is not an Imperial trap, and it's not Gerrera trying to bait us again.

CONTINUED

DRAVEN/CRACKEN PROG38906

HERE ARE THE FACTS:

- There's an Imperial defector on Jedha. Ensign Bodhi Rook, cargo pilot and Jedha native (see documentation). Recently stationed on Eadu. Claims knowledge of an Imperial "planet killer" and says he was sent by Dr. Galen Erso.
- The "planet killer" supposedly uses Jedha-mined kyber crystals. Might be why Rook defected there if it's on his cargo route. But, he's a Jedha native so he might have ties to Gerrera's gang. Or Galen Erso might have told him to find Gerrera. We don't know. We need more on Erso. Fast.
- I have an operative on Vulpter who can slice the Arakyd Industries data node; however, doing so will compromise her cover. We won't be able to use her a second time.

TO BE FAIR, THE INVESTIGATIONS ON GEONOSIS HAD BEEN LEADING US DOWN

I think it's worth it, but I need authorization immediately.

That was Saw's crusade. We didn't comprehend the debt we owed him until we could no longer repay it. —Leia

END DOCUMENT

DOC #2798799-ALL

TO: GEN. DRAVEN

FROM: CMDR. MON MOTHMA

SUBJ: VULPTER DATA RAID

Approved.

CLASSIFIED DOCUMENT—CLEARANCE LEVEL:

DRAVEN/CRACKEN PROG38991

RI 467-X1

VULPTER FINDINGS

TO: GENERAL CRACKEN

FROM: GENERAL DRAVEN

Project Celestial Power proved to be more than just kyber energy transformation. Its scientists tried to contain dark-matter quintessence. Wasn't required for the Death Star, but a dangerous line of research nonetheless.
-Statura

The raid paid off. Dr. Erso works for Krennic, on Project Celestial Power in particular. He joined up with the B'ankora division years ago to help Krennic solve the kyber crystal energy transformation sequence. He's a big fish.

From a Coruscant residential permit, we know that Galen Erso had a wife (Lyra) and a daughter (Jyn). We came up dry on Lyra's whereabouts but according to an old report from the Commenor Underground, a Jyn Erso was running with the resistance a decade ago.

First surprise? She was only twelve years old at the time. Second surprise? She was running with the Partisans under Saw Gerrera.

We're scrubbing the files for more on Jyn Erso, but the data on Dr. Galen Erso appears to tie together several different investigations: Project Celestial Power, the Tarkin Initiative, Dodonna's kyber research, and our superweapon speculation.

We need to get to Galen Erso and find out what he knows. I hate to say it, but it probably means playing nice with Saw Gerrera.

TWENTIES. I DON'T REMEMBER JYN ERSO. GERRERA WATCHED OVER HER VERY CLOSELY I THINK. - EMATT

MON MOTHMA TO GENERALS CRACKEN AND DRAVEN

Gentlemen, assuming the defector has already spilled his secrets to Saw Gerrera, I am skeptical we can get anything more out of him.

No, Gerrera won't share his knowledge with us, no matter how sweetly we beg. Who do we still have in his camp?

I might have made the same call. By this point, the waters had been poisoned.
—Leia

GENERAL DRAVEN TO COMMANDER MOTHMA AND GENERAL CRACKEN

No one we can trust. Not since Gerrera purged the ex-Frosthawks.

CLASSIFIED DOCUMENT—CLEARANCE LEVEL: 

CRACKEN/MOTHMA PROG40062

RI 553-B1

DEBRIEFING CAPT. ANDOR

TO: COMMANDER MOTHMA

FROM: GENERAL CRACKEN

Commander, Capt. Cassian Andor has returned from a mission to verify the facts of the Jedha situation. His contacts on the Ring of Kafrene confirmed Imperial trafficking in kyber crystals, with most shipments concealed in civilian convoys to hide the magnitude of whatever it is they're building.

(expand for full contents)

HENDRI UNDERHOLT

Commander, you asked me to coordinate intelligence reports. I hope you won't be disappointed that I've gone a step further.

HENDRI UNDERHOLT

With help from a friend in Intelligence, I assembled the attached report tracking the movements of Director Krennic and the frequency of his communications to Tarkin's Star Destroyer *Executrix* as well as to Tarkin's homeworld of Eriadu. Please see attachment YN-13.

MON MOTHMA

As always, Hendri, I am impressed by your drive, though I urge you to run similar initiatives by me in the future. As my aide you may wield my authority, but remember that you do not possess that authority yourself.

MON MOTHMA

I say this not to admonish you but to protect you. Politics is a toxic exercise. Even though all of us fight for a righteous cause, not everyone in the Alliance is your friend.

Building an alliance is thankless and perpetual. Even the New Republic Senate quickly split into Populists and Centrists. —Leia

DOC #3820035-ALL

TO: MON MOTHMA, ALLIANCE COMMANDER IN CHIEF

FROM: GENERAL DODONNA, SECTOR COMMAND

SUBJ: KYBER CRYSTALS

As you know, I've been working to map the kyber supply lines. Now that Captain Andor has confirmed Kafrene as a shipping hub, I remain confident that an area exists in the Unknown Regions where the weapon incorporating these crystals must be built. My earlier recommendations on assembly sites—Horuz and Patriim—should not be discarded, merely deemphasized.

If one kyber crystal can power a lightsaber, hundreds of thousands could form the backbone of an unimaginably powerful weapon. The critical factor is size.

Kyber crystals are inert until powered, but a reactor capable of powering so many at once would need to be exponentially larger than anything driving our largest command ships. You'd have to hollow out a moon to house it.

I've included schematics created by my team related to quantum crystallography and hyperspatial displacement.

They could be using the old Imperial infrastructure. —Holdo

Relevant. We still don't know how widely the First Order has spread throughout the Unknown Regions.

INTEL IS ON IT. —EMATT

X-WING SQUADRONS HAVE BEEN RUNNING RECON. —POE

MON MOTHMA TO GENERAL CRACKEN

Ever since the rebel council got a whiff of the Jedha situation, there hasn't been a moment when someone wasn't chattering in my ear. Senator Jebel thinks it's a trick. Hostis Ij is convinced that Lord Darth Vader is going to show up on our doorstep any moment now, brandishing a lightsaber.

I agree with Admiral Holdo. We're staring at the surface. The depths are vast. Admiral Ackbar

I feel this way every day. When you become a leader, there is the temptation to force everyone to think the way that you do. It would make the job far less exhausting. —Leia

MEETING MINUTES: BASE ONE
INVITEES: REBEL COUNCIL
SUBJ: IMPERIAL SUPERWEAPON

MON MOTHMA: You have all read the report that summarizes Intelligence's best estimate on the nature of this Imperial superweapon, as well as its power source and its focusing mechanism. I have gathered–

SENATOR VASPAR: Actually, I haven't read it yet. I definitely received it, but when it came through I was in the middle of–

MON MOTHMA: Senator, if you don't mind, we will proceed and you can catch up on your own time. General Draven?

GENERAL DRAVEN: Thank you, Commander. The Imperial defector on Jedha calls it a "planet killer." How literally should we take this? The–

GENERAL DODONNA: Such an interpretation is possible, General Draven. It's mathematics. If you generate sufficient power and concentrate it into a focused beam, the destructive output can be calculated on a scale–

SENATOR JEBEL: It's a trick, Commander. We're wasting our time chasing phantoms.

SENATOR PAMLO: I disagree with Senator Jebel. I believe the threat is real. But I also know we can accomplish so much more if we control the message. Let us spread news of this horror across every sympathetic newsnet before the Empire can spin it to their benefit.

GENERAL ONORAN: That would mean surrendering our greatest advantage. Right now the Empire doesn't know what we know. Why would we announce it?

SENATOR JEBEL: None of this matters. We're arguing about a fantasy. The Empire has us chasing our own tails.

GENERAL DRAVEN: And what if you're wrong? Suppose the threat is real. We have no counterattack. The Alliance would die in a single breath.

MON MOTHMA: One at a time, councillors. Thank you. Now please direct your attention to the hologram.

(see p. 2)

CLASSIFIED DOCUMENT—CLEARANCE LEVEL:

DELTO/DRAVEN PROG40108

RI 333-A5

GEONOSIS/ULTIMATE WEAPON

TO: GEN. DRAVEN

FROM: COL. DELTO

General:

Believe it or not, Geonosis might be relevant again. If it sounds like I'm joking, it's only because you know how many times we've pursued a Geonosis connection only to come up dry. But consider . . .

Fact: We know the Geonosians worked for the Separatists during the Clone Wars and designed a project explicitly labeled the "Ultimate Weapon" (according to secondhand documentation).

Fact: Abandoned construction modules, big enough to construct a large spacegoing weapon, still orbit Geonosis. If the Empire was building something there, they moved it long ago.

Fact: The Empire sterilized Geonosis with poison gas—as verified by the Phoenix mission a couple years back—exterminating hive engineers by the millions. Almost as if they wanted to cover something up.

No, I'm not exactly breaking new ground here, but the new revelations about kyber crystals forced me to take a second look at the data. The Geonosian hives leaned heavily into crystalline research of their own, importing magmatic crystals by the ton. They even outsourced one offshoot—code name Hammertong—to a facility on the crystal planet of Mygeeto.

Although most of the Geonosis data is more than twenty years old, I'm convinced that it bears some relevance to our current puzzle.

NOTE: LOOK INTO HAMMERTONG. THE LONGER THE RUMORS OF A FIRST ORDER SUPERWEAPON PERSIST, THE MORE I'M CONVINCED THERE'S SOMETHING TO THEM. - EMATT

GENERAL DODONNA to COMMANDER MOTHMA

Commander, with the last of the comm stations unpacked in Operations (not installed yet but by end of day tomorrow without a doubt), I am happy to announce that we have officially moved in. Welcome to the new Base One. Let us hope Yavin 4 remains our home longer than Dantooine did.

But the heat! Dantooine's climate was at least tolerable on good days. —Leia

HOT, SWEATY. AND THE INSECTS! - EMATT

RECON FILE

YAVIN 4

SECTOR: Gordian Reach

REGION: Outer Rim Territories

ORBITAL SHELL: 4 of 26

DIAMETER: 10,200 km

BIOME: Jungle

PRIMARY HYPERLANES: Hydian Way

TRACE HYPERLANES: Pinooran Spur, Junction-Tierrel Loop, Yavin Bypass

LANDMASS A: Starloft

LANDMASS B: Weytin

Massassi ruin complex

Great Temple/Base One HQ

Active and reserve pilots from Gold, Blue, Green, Red Squadrons to operate throughout greater Gordian

NOTE: Details of the gas giant's orbital shells are not recorded in Imperial star charts as of Nav Guild release 5570.A6.

—prepared by Lt. Dr'uun Unnh

BASE ONE

YAVIN 4

WE RAN OUT OF COTS IN THE BARRACKS, AS I RECALL. SOME OF US FASHIONED HAMMOCKS OUT OF CARGO NETS. – EMATT

LEVEL 1: HANGAR BAY, FUSION GENERATORS, ARMORY, SICK BAY, MACHINE SHOP

LEVEL 2: WAR ROOM, STOREHOUSES, TECHNICAL WORKSHOPS, DROID REPAIR, BARRACKS, COMMISSARY, SENSOR SUITES

LEVEL 3: COMMAND CENTER, OFFICERS' QUARTERS, SECURITY STATION, ANALYSIS LABS, RECOVERY WARD, COMMUNICATIONS

LEVEL 4: GRAND AUDIENCE CHAMBER/STORAGE

DOC #3822235-ALL

TO: MON MOTHMA, ALLIANCE COMMANDER IN CHIEF
FROM: GENERAL DODONNA, SECTOR COMMAND
SUBJ: X-WING FLIGHT PATROL SCHEDULE

For your review. Flight patrol schedule prepared by Col. Cor.

PATROL ROUTE:
Yavin to Gordian Trace Relays (coreward, spinward, rimward).

MISSION:
Perform flyby of surrounding space. After verifying visual and sensor all clear, perform close uplink of passive relay recordings.

DIDN'T REALIZE THE T-65s COULDN'T LINK FROM LONG RANGE? THIS SEEMS REALLY DANGEROUS, LEAVING THE PILOT VULNERABLE TO DETECTION AND AMBUSH. NO WONDER THEY SENT THEM OUT IN PAIRS. -POE

SHIFT CYCLE 1:
Red Leader (Cmdr. Garven Dreis) and Red 11 (Maj. Ralo Surrel)

SHIFT CYCLE 2:
Red 7 (Cdt. Harb Binli) and Red 5 (Cdt. Pedrin Gaul), accompanied by Red 9 (Lt. Nozzo Naytaan)

SHIFT CYCLE 3:
Green 4 (Lt. Attico Wred) and Green 12 (Lt. Wion Dillems)

DOC #3854446-ALL

TO: MON MOTHMA, ALLIANCE COMMANDER IN CHIEF
FROM: GENERAL MERRICK, STARFIGHTER COMMAND
SUBJ: WHEN SHOULD WE USE THE U-WING?

OFFICIAL DOCUMENT

Commander, thanks to Sen. Organa, we'll soon have enough U-wings to fill out a squadron or two at Base One. I think this is a good time to evaluate the craft's role within Starfighter Command.

We never got this many, of that I can be sure. After Scarif they were even scarcer. Admiral Ackbar

CONTINUED

With the approval of Gen. Dodonna and Col. Cor, and with the input of the pilots who have logged the most U-wing flight time, I have prepared the following recommendation.

ROLE: Multipurpose. To date, the Alliance has deployed the U-wing as:

- Troop transport (at Mantooine)
- Gunship (in support of the Tocan system extraction)
- Medevac lifter (during the retreat from Gaulus)
- As a cargo and VIP escort (between Mon Cala and Telaris and points coreward)

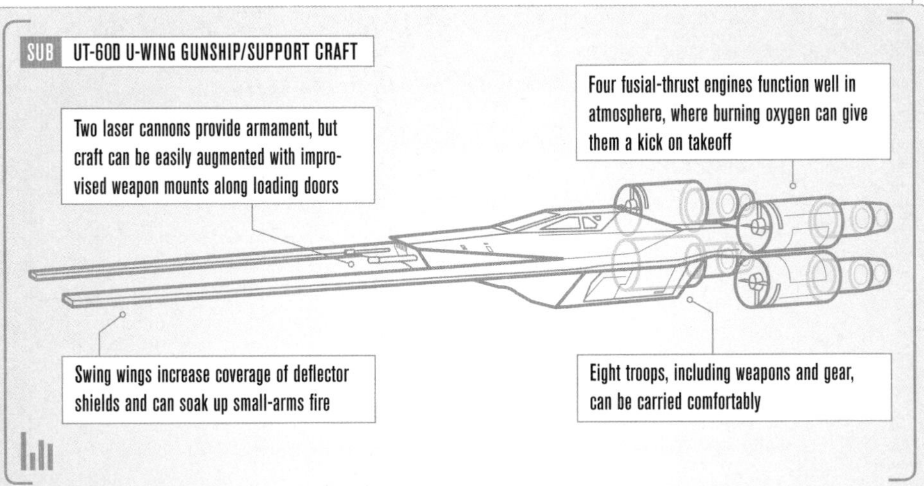

RECOMMENDATION: The first three roles are viable. The fourth is redundant. We should cycle the U-wing out of escort duty, away from any mission in which starfighter combat is probable due to its wide turn radius and slow acceleration. That role should instead be filled by X-wings and A-wings. Y-wings are less suitable but are still a better match than U-wings for ship-to-ship combat.

General Onoran says the Pathfinders have grown fond of the ship. Now that we're settled into our new HQ, we should consider allocating future U-wing shipments to both Starfighter Command and Special Forces.

END DOCUMENT

SMART ASSESSMENT, BUT THIS IS ANTOC MERRICK WE'RE TALKING ABOUT. HE COULD OUTFLY MOST PILOTS WHO'VE EVER LIVED. -POE

BAIL ORGANA TO MON MOTHMA, GENERAL CRACKEN

As you can see, I'm trying to keep the Empire off my scent. When they encounter these same U-wings in combat, however . . .

I appreciate any help that Rebel Intelligence can offer in further obscuring Alderaan's link to the missing shipment.

My father's role did not go unnoticed, though the Senate provided some diplomatic protection from the ISB. —Leia

If I may, it seemed easier to steal from a hostile government back then than to request assets from a friendly one today. —Holdo

Regretfully, I agree. —Leia

TO: Chief Investigator Axvering, Imperial Security Bureau
FROM: Imperial Senator Bail Organa, Alderaan Sector
SUBJ: UT-60D shipment

Investigator Axvering—while I hold the deepest respect for your office, I question whether my numerous answers concerning the missing cargo of UT-60D U-wings are ultimately an effective use of your time.

As I stated in response to your initial query, the shipment departed as planned from Aldraig in the Alderaan sector. I also understand that no record exists of the shipment's arrival on Coruscant.

Are you certain the confusion doesn't lie with the Coruscant port authority? Perhaps the shipment was merely mislogged.

I have acknowledged that a data clerk on Aldraig mistakenly routed the shipment through Baylagon, but one extra layover is barely an inconvenience for a competent cargo pilot.

Nonetheless, I apologize again for the routing error. The Royal House of Alderaan is prepared to compensate the Empire for the cost of the additional fuel.

Sincerely,
Senator Bail Organa

SENATOR VASPAR TO COMMANDER MOTHMA

Mon Mothma— A member of my security detail shared these sketches made by a Corporal Mefran of SpecForces. They depict hazardous wildlife lurking in the jungles of this moon. That this danger has been withheld from us is genuinely alarming. I demand to know what steps you are taking to ensure the safety of everyone at this base.

CONTINUED

DOC ATTACHMENT #00421

SENATOR VASPAR TO COMMANDER MOTHMA

Four-winged flyer (easily as big as me) with a wickedly hooked beak. It flew away when I got close, but when it spread its wings, its coloration bloomed, going from deep blue to bright orange in an instant.

Each one of these shiny-shelled crawlers was about the size of my fist. They've already done some superficial damage to the base of our watchtower near the southern lagoon. Nothing serious, but we should keep an eye on it.

2

END

COMMANDER MOTHMA TO SENATOR VASPAR

Senator—you are inside a security perimeter and surrounded by hundreds of trained fighters. I am confident you will agree that, at the present time, preventative animal control takes a lower priority than our fight against the Empire.

Thank you for sharing the drawings, however. The herd mother is my favorite.

HENDRI UNDERHOLT

Mon Mothma—I've been trying to manage your daily schedule since we arrived on Yavin 4 so you wouldn't have to deal with the endless requests. Now I'm worried that I've been leaving you out of the loop. Sen. Vaspar keeps telling me that he requires your ear, naming various projects and important people that I don't know. I apologize in advance if I have handled this badly.

MON MOTHMA

There is a powerful weapon feared by bureaucrats and bullies everywhere. The weapon is "no." Hendri, you have my trust. You may speak on my behalf. If something is truly important, I'll know.

And though you might phrase it as "You cannot see the commander at this time," I quite like "no." It's honest and direct. Use it well.

Far more important than political grooming, far more useful than combat training. This outlook is everything. —Leia

GENERAL DRAVEN TO COMMANDER MOTHMA

Thought you might want to see this, as this is the unit that had that run-in with the droids belonging to Senator Organa's pilot. The senator isn't one to complain, but others around the base are starting to.

DROID POOL: UNIT MAINTENANCE

TECHNICIAN: HARISHA GULAN

UNIT: K-2SO

MANUFACTURER: ARAKYD INDUSTRIES

BACKGROUND:

This specialized KX security droid has been reformatted under the direction by Capt. Cassian Andor of Rebel Intelligence.

END

The reformatting overrode its factory-installed inhibitors. The droid exhibits erratic and antisocial behavior.

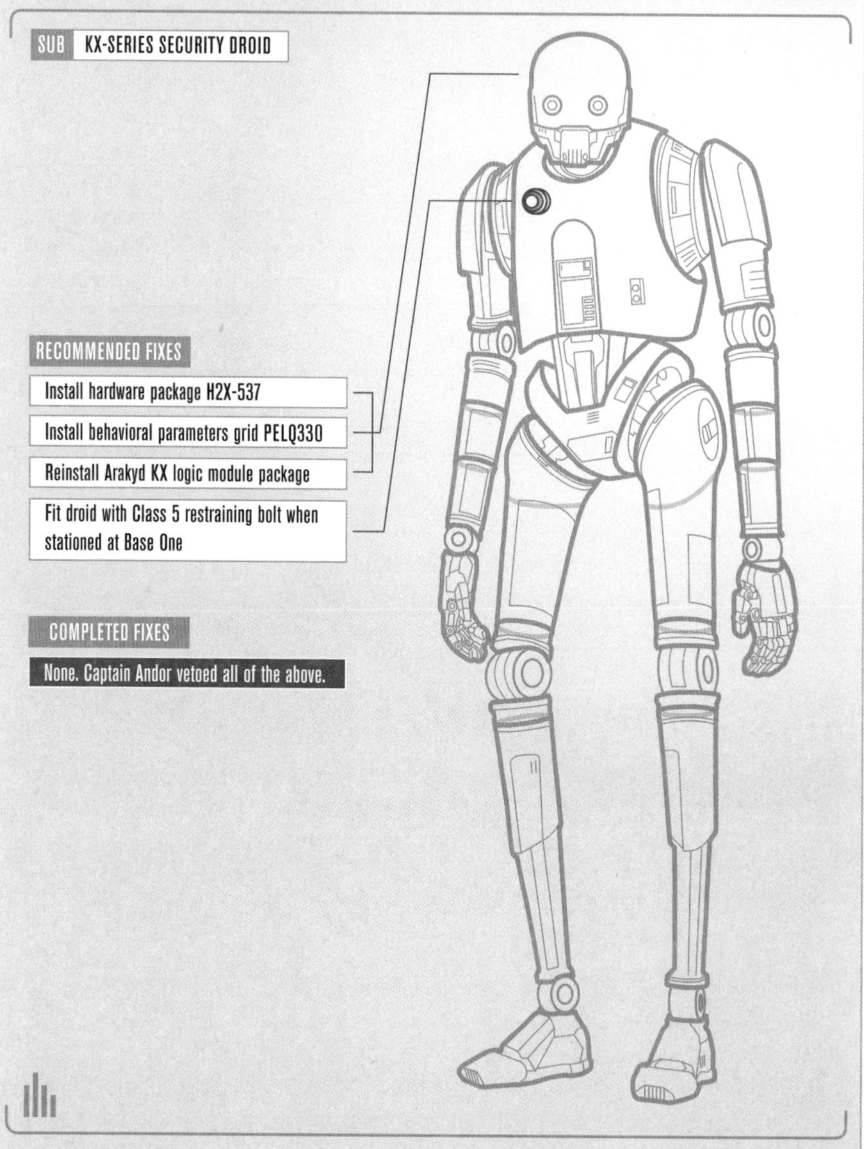

END

DOC #4115325-ALL

TO: ALLIANCE INTELLIGENCE: CRACKEN, DRAVEN

FROM: MON MOTHMA

SUBJ: SUPERWEAPON CONSTRUCTION FOOTPRINTS

OFFICIAL DOCUMENT

Generals, if the Empire's superweapon incorporates a power source anywhere close to the magnitude that you're speculating, its reactor and surrounding superstructure will be positively gargantuan. Any project on that scale will leave footprints.

Very similar to the approach we must take in pursuing leads on the First Order superweapon. –Statura

Starting immediately, please provide regular reports on:

- **Supply lines.** Laminasteel, quadanium, rhodium, etc. The Empire requires vast quantities of rare resources, all of them trackable. The supply lines are out there, no matter how many redirects they've inserted into the middle.

THE UNKNOWN REGIONS ARE VAST. – EMATT

- **Talent sourcing.** General laborers (either organics or droids) will make a ripple through sheer numbers. Skilled laborers and specialists are needed in much smaller quantities, but their families and colleagues must have insights into their classified employment.
- **Orbital construction sites.** Even if we've eliminated a system from consideration, what does that tell us? Why did the Empire abandon Geonosis?

So this is how we narrow it down. We can't wait for the First Order to make the first move. –Statura

DOC #4235335-ALL

TO: CMDR. MOTHMA

FROM: GEN. CRACKEN

SUBJ: TWO NEW LEADS (SPECULATIVE)

Passing on the latest from Maj. Harinar and Col. Delto. I've allowed their teams to operate independently, theorizing the most likely configuration that a kyber superweapon would take. As you will see, they arrived at very different conclusions.

CONTINUED

DOC 0321842

HARINAR TO CRACKEN: OPERATION CINDER

We've been sitting on an intercepted Imperial transmission concerning Operation Cinder and have collected enough corroborating evidence to suggest it's some sort of climate disruption array.

If levels of energy efficiency similar to Project Celestial Power were applied to such a device, you'd have a satellite that could trigger planetary heatwaves and boil entire oceans. It would legitimately be a planet killer.

Was used for posthumous, nihilistic destruction by Palpatine. He targeted Commenor, Candovant, Vardos, and other planets including his own homeworld of Naboo. I couldn't have stopped it without Lieutenant Bey. —Leia

I KNEW MOM WAS A GREAT PILOT, BUT WOW! -POE

DOC 0322352

DELTO TO CRACKEN: SIEGE BREAKER

Maybe I lack the Empire's taste for catastrophe? I'm just not convinced you need a moon-sized reactor to power a kyber crystal cannon. A Jedi lightsaber, after all, could cut through nearly any material while still fitting comfortably inside a satchel.

Should the Empire abandon theatrics, it could build a thousand small cannons for the cost of a single "planet killer." Versatile, portable cannons that could shatter mountains and crack all but the strongest energy shields.

PERHAPS THIS IS WHAT THE FIRST ORDER IS UP TO? WOULD REPRESENT A MORE CONTAINABLE RISK. - EMATT

END DOCUMENT

MEETING MINUTES: BASE ONE
INVITEES: REBEL COUNCIL
SUBJ: OPERATION FRACTURE

MON MOTHMA: The goal is to recover Dr. Galen Erso from the Empire or to secure the details of his research concerning the Imperial planet killer.

SENATOR PAMLO: If the extraction is successful, Senator Organa and I will bring Dr. Erso before the Senate to testify about the Empire's crimes.

GENERAL DRAVEN: Let me remind the council that Dr. Erso is an Imperial collaborator. Recovery is the ideal outcome, but it may become necessary to eliminate this asset and deprive the Empire of Erso's expertise. If they have not yet completed the primary weapon–

SENATOR PAMLO: We are not assassins, General.

GENERAL DRAVEN: We are soldiers, Senator.

MON MOTHMA: This is not the forum for this particular debate. Recovery of Dr. Erso or his information is the purpose of Operation Fracture. General Draven, please outline your plan.

GENERAL DRAVEN: We've located Dr. Erso's daughter, Jyn Erso, in an Imperial labor camp in the Wobani system. We believe that she served with Saw Gerrera's Partisans as recently as–

SENATOR JEBEL: Stop right there. We should want nothing to do with Gerrera's Partisans.

MON MOTHMA: No one is more aware of Saw's crimes than I, Senator. However, if this Imperial defector is inside Gerrera's camp on Jedha, then Jyn Erso could be our envoy to the hostiles.

SENATOR VASPAR: And why would she cooperate with us?

MON MOTHMA: Freedom from prison, for a start. We will consider other incentives if necessary. General Draven, perhaps you can outline the Wobani operation.

(see p. 2)

CONFIRMED: THIS IS JYN ERSO. SUBJECT HAS ALSO USED THE ALIASES OF LYRA RALLIK, KESTREL DAWN, TANITH PONTA, AND NARI MCVEE.

—CAPT. ANDOR

IMPERIAL ENFORCEMENT DATACORE
PRISON INTAKE FORM
WOBANI LABOR COLONY

SUBJECT: Hallik, Liana

AGE: 22 standard years (estimated)

SPECIES: Human

HEIGHT: 1.6 meters

SITE OF ARREST: Corulag

CLASSIFIED DOCUMENT—CLEARANCE LEVEL: 

DRAVEN/MOTHMA PROG40099

RI 098-X5

INTEL UPDATE CIC: WOBANI EXTRACTION, EXTRACTION TEAM BRAVO

TO: COMMANDER MOTHMA

FROM: GENERAL DRAVEN

Commander—Below is Sergeant Melshi's plan for extracting Jyn Erso from Wobani. Melshi has assembled a strike team composed of our best SpecForce fighters under Team Bravo. On the recommendation of Captain Andor, he's also bringing the droid.

MISSION: Extraction of "Liana Hallik"

TARGET: Imperial labor camp and penal colony, Wobani

FILED BY: Sgt. Ruescott Melshi, SpecForces

Stage 1: Atmospheric insertion and sensor evasion; U-wing touchdown at coordinates 34.2127, 122.3808

Stage 2: Squad disembarks and proceeds under cover to Ambush Point A

Stage 3: Impede progress of prisoner transport halfway between prison and work detail

Stage 4: See diagram

As I've stated many times, we lack the ground vehicles needed to take the fight to the First Order during planetary assaults. This mission could serve as the template for stocking our pool. – EMATT

HENDRI UNDERHOLT

Commander, I just returned from the chamber where Jyn Erso is being held. She's still in shackles. Is this how we treat our recruits? Why should she trust us?

MON MOTHMA

I will take it under advisement, Hendri.

HENDRI UNDERHOLT

Thank you, Commander. The Alliance should represent a better way forward.

RI 544-X2

INTEL UPDATE CIC: STRIKE TEAM (RAPID RESPONSE)

TO: COMMANDER MOTHMA

FROM: GENERAL DRAVEN

Commander— If Jyn Erso can't get the job done, we need to consider a plan for raiding Saw Gerrera's fortress in the Jedha catacombs.

Most of these are bios you've seen before. It takes genuine fearlessness (or foolishness) to rush in against long odds, but those who also possess self-awareness stand a chance of remaining alive past the first minute.

I recommend we begin with these soldiers and build a larger squad around them.

Corporal Pao
Commando

Corporal Timker
Fortifications

Corporal Stordan Tonc
Infantry

Corporal Mefran
Wilderness

Corporal Casrich
Commando

Corporal Maddel
Urban scout

Corporal Bistan
Gunner

Corporal Rostok
Sniper

Private Basteren
Spotter

Private Kapperil
Recon

Private Calfor
Demolitions

DRAVEN WAS ON TO SOMETHING. AT SCARIF, HOWEVER, THESE SOLDIERS WEREN'T ASSIGNED. THEY VOLUNTEERED FOR AN UNSANCTIONED MISSION.

– EMATT

DOC #44442035-ALL

TO: CMDR. MOTHMA

FROM: GEN. DRAVEN

SUBJ: OPERATION FRACTURE STAGE TWO

For your review: stage two of Operation Fracture.

Capt. Andor will accompany Jyn Erso to Jedha to protect the Alliance's interests. Andor is also bringing the droid, who may prove necessary should Erso try to escape. I have authorized a U-wing for their use.

Additionally, I have given Capt. Andor secondary mission objectives. Jedha represents an opportunity to gather intel on Gerrera's new crew and also lets us observe the kyber supply chain up close.

COMMANDER—MESSAGE RECEIVED FROM CAPTAIN ANDOR ON JEDHA.

WEAPON CONFIRMED

HOLY CITY DESTROYED

MISSION TARGET LOCATED ON EADU

PLEASE ADVISE

Losing the Holy City seemed inconceivable, until Alderaan. It is discouraging to expect better of your enemies and to be proven wrong. —Leia

CLASSIFIED DOCUMENT—CLEARANCE LEVEL:

DRAVEN/MERRICK PROG40288

RI 443-B4

BLUE SQUADRON SCRAMBLE

TO: GENERAL MERRICK

FROM: GENERAL DRAVEN

TARGET: Imperial research facility on Eadu (see supplementary materials for coordinates)

OBJECTIVE: Hit-and-fade raid. Destroy the encampment. Level all structures. Eliminate all defenders.

FROM WHAT I KNOW, BLUE SQUADRON FLEW IN ALMOST BLIND WITH NO TIME TO PREP. WITH EADU'S WEATHER BEING WHAT IT IS, IT'S AMAZING THEY MADE IT OUT ALIVE. -POE

CONTINUED

DRAVEN/MERRICK PROG40288

RECON FILE

Eadu

REGION: Outer Rim Territories

DIAMETER: 14,121 km

ATMOSPHERE: Storms (high precipitation, high winds, electrical discharges)

TARGET: Tarkin Initiative laboratories

TARGET DEFENSES: Antiaircraft turbolasers, TIE squadron

END DOCUMENT

TRINEBULON NEWS

The Truth, Straight from the Source

MINING CATASTROPHE

Illegal Practices End in Disaster, Survivors in Shock

Jedha—A report issued this morning to members of the Imperial Senate confirmed the destruction of the Holy City of Jedha and blamed the catastrophe on outlaw miners, sources say.

Jedha, one of the few sources of kyber crystals in the galaxy, has long attracted illegal diggers. But an increased Imperial presence wasn't enough to halt their actions entirely. Yesterday's explosion of a storehouse containing megonite and baradium wiped out the Holy City with a death toll estimated in the hundreds of thousands.

"Regulations exist for a reason, and there is no clearer example than what we have just witnessed on Jedha," said Governor Sacritte in remarks released exclusively to *TriNebulon News*.

Many ~~believed this explanation at the time. Some still believe it. After all these years, I still don't~~ know how to fight denial. —Leia

SENATOR PAMLO TO COMMANDER MOTHMA

We should have acted at once and now it's too late. Had we gotten word out to the galaxy of the Empire's superweapon, the massacre at Jedha would have been proof of our claims. Instead the Empire has been allowed to frame this as an industrial accident. The truth now seems outlandish in comparison.

Winning a war isn't just about soldiers and starships. We need to start controlling the narrative.

I clashed with Senator Pamlo at the time, being young and eager for a fight. I could use someone like Pamlo now. —Leia

HENDRI UNDERHOLT

I know you must be frustrated at how the council meeting deteriorated into angry shouting. I admire you for keeping a level head.

HENDRI UNDERHOLT

But the interventionists are right. We should try to recover the Death Star plans on Scarif. I believe Jyn Erso. I know you do too.

CLASSIFIED DOCUMENT—CLEARANCE LEVEL: 

DRAVEN/MERRICK PROG40315

RI 443-B4

BLUE SQUADRON SCRAMBLE

TO: GENERAL MERRICK

FROM: GENERAL DRAVEN

Here's what we could pull together on Scarif on short notice:

- Map of citadel spire and surrounding area, annotated by our team
- Requisition order from a General Ramda concerning Scarif's defenses (possibly several months out of date)
- Schedule for Scarif planetary shield gate

We could provide more if we had more time, but . . .

The planner's lament. -Statura

CONTINUED

RECON FILE

Scarif

REGION: Outer Rim Territories

DIAMETER: 9,112 km

SATELLITES: None

TERRAIN: Volcanic island chains

RESOURCES: Dense metals used in starship construction

ESTIMATED POPULATION: 475,000

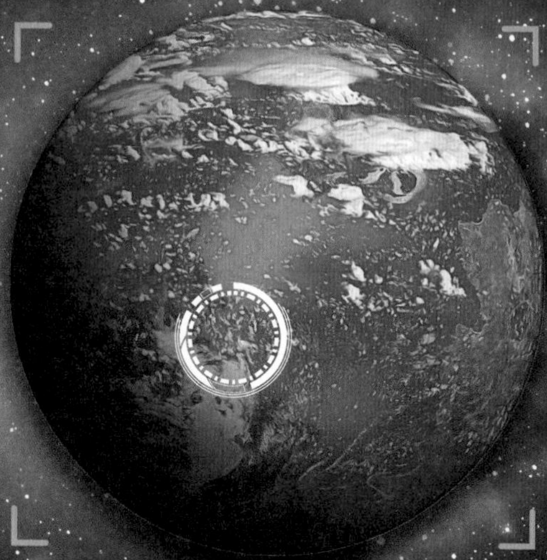

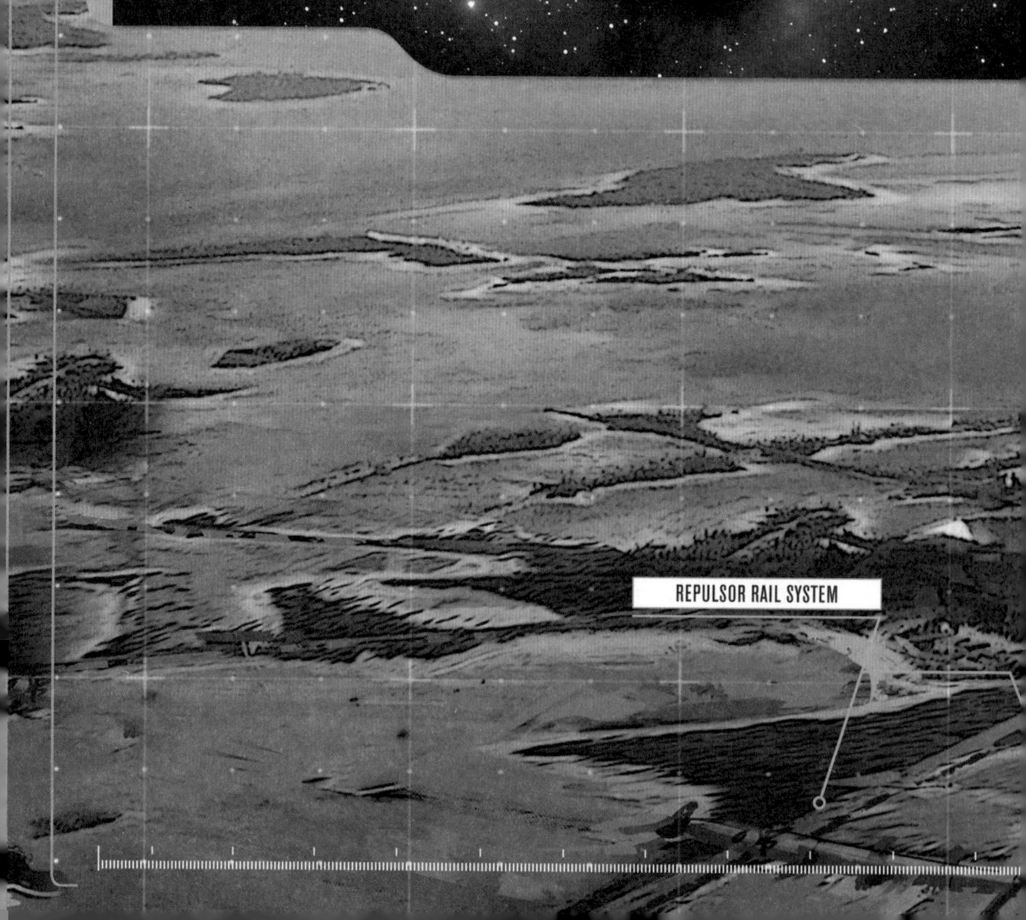

REPULSOR RAIL SYSTEM

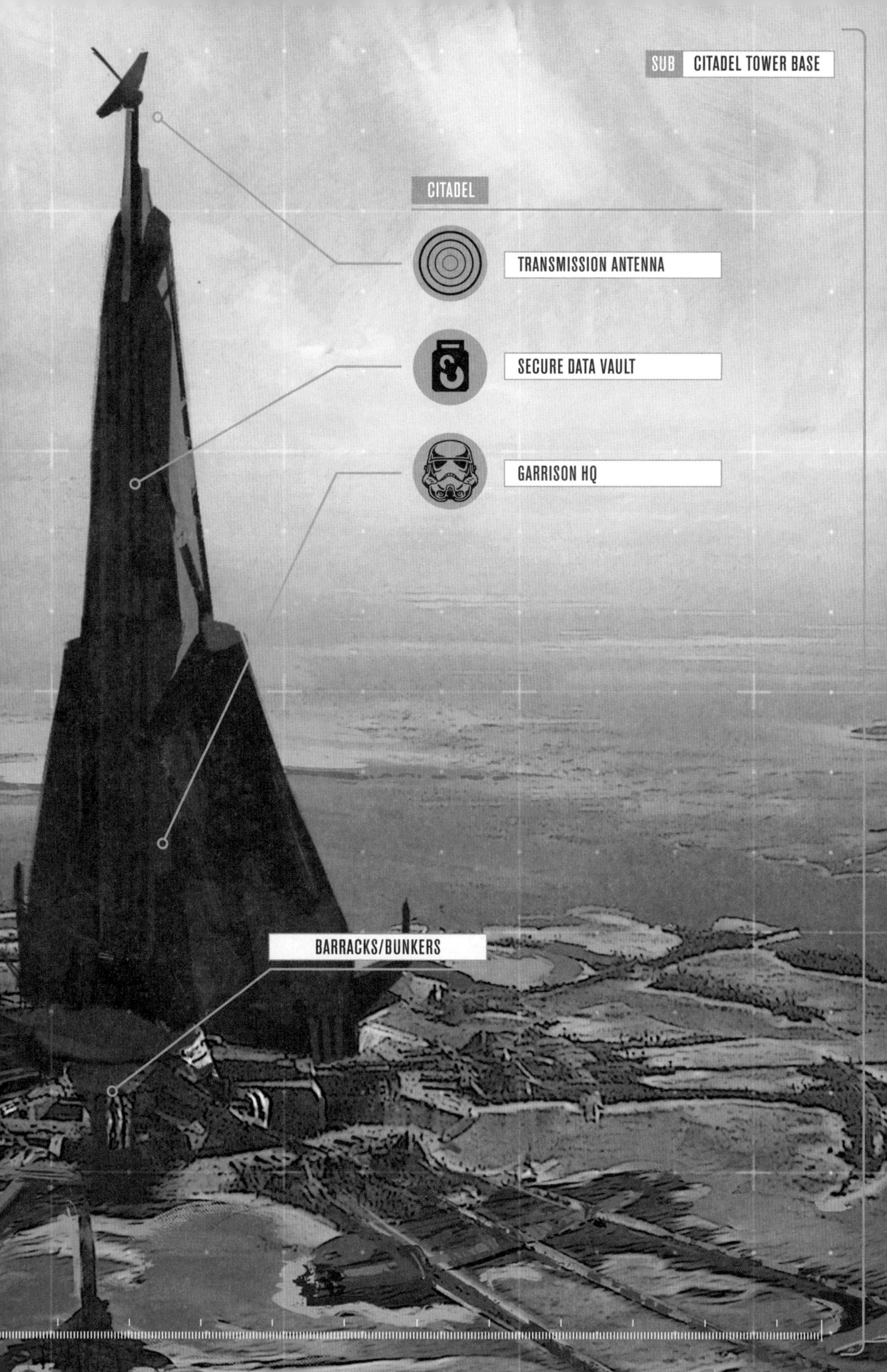
SUB
CITADEL TOWER BASE
CITADEL
TRANSMISSION ANTENNA
SECURE DATA VAULT
GARRISON HQ
BARRACKS/BUNKERS

ALLIANCE DECRYPT V54//DELTO//SUBSPACE TRANSCEIVER INTERCEPT

INTERCEPTED TRANSMISSION

From: General Sotorus Ramda
To: Lieutenant Berretic
Re: Scarif defenses

Rewrite this request using the official formatting and send it up through the Oversector until someone listens. NOT TARKIN. One of the sector admirals. Tarkin has the Emperor's ear and thus we must present our best face to him at all times.

Here's what I'm requesting:

- TIE strikers (two squadrons): We recently loaned these squadrons to the *Unassailable*. I want them back. The TIE/sk is ideal for atmospheric patrolling, and our pilots and bombardiers need them for flight training.
- AT-ACTs (twelve): Needed to transport ore between mines and refineries.
- Shoretroopers (two companies): Scarif is one of the only worlds in the sector suitable for shoretroopers, so I can't imagine the use they are serving aboard Star Destroyers.
- Death troopers (two platoons): The training camp requires additional instructors. I'd prefer veterans with body augmentations at v1.01 or earlier.

ALL TIES HANDLE POORLY IN ATMOSPHERE EXCEPT THESE. THE EMPIRE SHOULD HAVE MADE A LOT MORE, IF ONLY FOR USE AS GARRISON DETACHMENTS. -POE

NOT ARMORED FOR COMBAT, DESPITE THE ACRONYM. MORE THAN ENOUGH AGAINST INFANTRY HOWEVER. -EMATT

INTERCEPTED TRANSMISSION

SCARIF SHIELD GATE
GOLAN M3185
SPREAD: GLOBAL
MAGNITUDE: 50
RIGIDITY: 50
FREQUENCY PATTERN: OVERLAPPING SHELL

ORBITAL COMMAND: ADM. GORIN
SURFACE COMMAND: GEN. RAMDA

CARGO TRAFFIC WILL BE PERMITTED THROUGH SHIELD GATE FROM 0600–1100 AND 1400–2100
MAINTAIN PARKING ORBIT AS DIRECTED BY SHIELD GATE OTC
ONLY VESSELS WITH ACTIVE SECURITY CODES WILL BE PERMITTED ENTRY

CLASSIFIED DOCUMENT—CLEARANCE LEVEL: 

RADDUS/MOTHMA PROG40323

RI 038-F1

REBEL FLEET

TO: COMMANDER MOTHMA

FROM: ADMIRAL RADDUS

Commander, by the time you read this we'll already be on our way.

I'm still scrambling fleet elements, but by the time we arrive at Scarif, I hope to command:

- The *Profundity*
- 2 Nebulon-B frigates
- 3-4 Hammerhead corvettes
- 2-4 Dornean gunships
- 5-10 Corellian corvettes
- 12 medium transports
- Miscellaneous freighters, gunships, and support craft

May the Force be with us.

That cloudy-eyed old fish! To think that he called this school an armada. Admiral Ackbar

You commanded multiple small vessels at Endor, did you not, Admiral? -Statura

More than one heavy battleship, Statura. More than one! Admiral Ackbar

MON MOTHMA TO BAIL ORGANA

Per our discussion, Leia will take the *Tantive IV* to Tatooine to collect Jedi Master Obi-Wan Kenobi from his exile. With the Death Star now a terrifying reality, Master Kenobi's insight is essential to the success of our anti-Imperial insurgency.

DOC #4832146-ALL

TO: CMDR. MOTHMA

FROM: GEN. DRAVEN

SUBJ: SCARIF AFTERMATH

We've lost contact with the *Tantive IV*. The *Tantive IV*'s initial

CONTINUED

DOC #4832146-ALL

transmission confirmed their escape from Scarif with the Death Star plans aboard and stated that they intended to leverage the diplomatic protection of Senator Leia Organa to bypass Imperial patrols.

Since then, we have intercepted two transmissions. The first, a coded narrow-beam subspace alert concerning Imperial pursuit in the Tatooine system, and less than an hour later, a distress call broadcast across all sector traffic channels claiming catastrophic damage in an asteroid collision.

I don't have to tell you that the latter transmission is almost certainly an Imperial fake. From this, we can presume that the *Tantive IV* has been captured or destroyed.

We are doing everything we can to verify the vessel's status, including activating all Intelligence agents on Tatooine.

I wish I had better news.

END DOCUMENT

I survived as a prisoner, first aboard Vader's Star Destroyer and then aboard the Death Star. I never learned the fates of the others. —Leia

DOC #4992146-ALL

TO: CMDR. MOTHMA

FROM: GEN. DODONNA

SUBJ: DEATH STAR IMAGES/FLEET UPDATE

OFFICIAL DOCUMENT

Just before the Battle of Scarif, one of our Far Needle pilots encountered the Death Star near the jumping-off point to the Terrabe Bypass and captured a scan. We've combined this scan with the data recorded by our fleet sensors at Scarif.

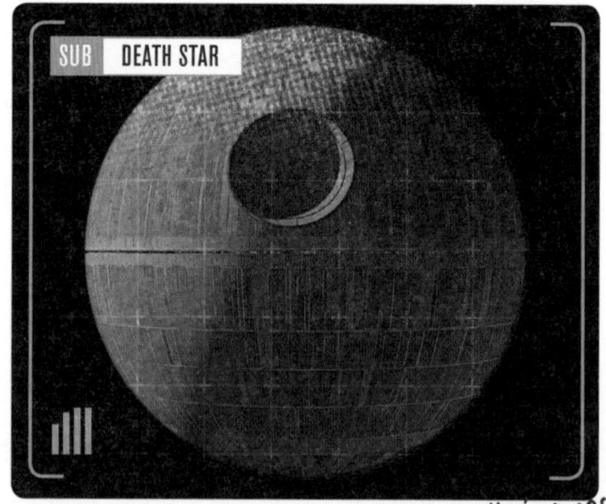

In other news, Col. Zavor has established contact with Ackbar and the remaining fleet elements. Expect a status report soon.

Shorthanded, behind schedule, underequipped, and hardly in a position to supplant Raddus and bolster the rebel fleet. I am grateful my actual report is not reproduced in this archiv[e] —Admiral Ackbar

THE FAINT HOPE THAT WE MIGHT EXPOSE THE DEATH STAR BEFORE THE SENATE AND SPUR POLITICAL REFORMATION IS NOW DEAD. EMPEROR PALPATINE HAS DISSOLVED THAT BODY, EFFECTIVE IMMEDIATELY.

PAMLO, VASPAR, AND JEBEL ARE IN A PANIC, AND SEEKING REFUGE ON AN ALLIANCE SAFE WORLD. THOUGH I HAVE SENT SEVERAL COMMUNICATIONS TO BAIL, I HAVE HEARD NOTHING FROM ALDERAAN.

THE EMPEROR'S UNELECTED GOVERNORS NOW CONTROL THE GALAXY'S SECTORS. NO ONE SPEAKS FOR CHANDRILA OR ANY OF A THOUSAND OTHER WORLDS. SOME POPULATIONS ARE ESPECIALLY VULNERABLE, IN PARTICULAR THE MON CAL, THE SULLUSTANS, THE DRESSELIANS. WE SHOULD PLAN TO TAKE IN REFUGEES.

A forward-thinking move, and one that swelled our ranks in the subsequent months. Brought in some badly needed tech specialists as well. —Leia

WHY WOULD PALPATINE DO THIS? THE SENATE WAS LARGELY HIS TO CONTROL, A PUPPET LEGISLATURE THAT GAVE HIS REGIME THE SURFACE SHEEN OF FAIRNESS. THAT HE NO LONGER REQUIRES EVEN THE <u>ILLUSION</u> OF DEBATE IS OMINOUS.

I WAS WRONG. THE DEATH STAR IS NO MERE DETERRENT. THE EMPIRE HAS USED IT TWICE NOW, AT JEDHA AND SCARIF.

THE GALAXY HAS ENTERED INTO A NEW AND TERRIFYING REALITY WHERE PALPATINE'S OFFER IS PLAIN. OBEY HIM, OR DIE.

CLASSIFIED DOCUMENT—CLEARANCE LEVEL:

CRACKEN/MOTHMA PROG40134

RI 0065-X5

INTEL UPDATE CIC: DISSOLUTION OF THE IMPERIAL SENATE

TO: COMMANDER MOTHMA

FROM: GENERAL CRACKEN

Commander—Palpatine just tossed a thermal detonator into the heart of our Intelligence apparatus.

CONTINUED

CRACKEN/MOTHMA PROG40134

Most of our Coruscant operatives—senators, aides, ambassadors, even pages—no longer have any political power, not under this new structure. We've been silenced.

Imperial Intelligence will use this event as an excuse to arrest the most outspoken politicians. Interrogations will soon follow. Where is Senator Organa?

I'm attaching a reprioritized list of Imperial contacts. We've got to rebuild our network.

INTEL TO PENETRATE THE EMPIRE'S EXECUTIVE BRANCH. SO MANY NEW FACES. - EMATT

END DOCUMENT

DOC #4995660-ALL

TO: CMDR. MOTHMA
FROM: GEN. CRACKEN
SUBJ: IMPERIAL TRANSMISSION

Colonel Delto has a rare find: a high-priority Imperial communique relayed through the package we installed in the holonet satellite near Plympto. Romodi is a general in the Imperial Army, attached to the Death Star's command staff and highly favored by Palpatine. And you already know Tarkin.

ALLIANCE DECRYPT V55.4//DELTO//SKIFTER SAT INTERCEPT

From: General Romodi
To: Grand Moff Tarkin
Re: Data breach

The actions at Scarif have proven insufficient. That we have suffered further leakage from the Tatooine intercept cannot be ruled out at this time.

We must take immediate action to neutralize political and military opposition.

I may be the only living person who saw it happen. Who witnessed it with my own eyes and had to live with the memory.
—Leia

GENERAL CRACKEN TO COMMANDER MOTHMA

Alderaan. You saw the report. I am heartsick to tell you that it's true. We have received no word from Bail Organa or his retinue. We have no indication that he survived the catastrophe. No further updates on the *Tantive IV* or the Death Star plans at this time.

SENATOR PAMLO TO COMMANDER MOTHMA

We have to tell the galaxy. The Empire can't ignore this, and there's no way they can spin it to their advantage. The Senate is gone, but the people still have ears! It's not too late to prevent further massacres.

The mourning is endless: my father, my mother, my friends, my city, my world. Every time I fail, I fail them. And no victory is great enough to ever bring them back.
—Leia

HENDRI UNDERHOLT

I've been fielding a lot of requests from people asking to meet with you about Alderaan. I've been saying that you're in private consultations, but I know you're in your quarters. I can see you haven't commed anyone. Tell me what I can do to help.

HENDRI UNDERHOLT

People need your leadership. Should we retreat or fight? Retaliate or go underground? You know how the council is. They'll stay deadlocked unless you step in.

HENDRI UNDERHOLT

You haven't eaten. I can bring something up from the commissary. Answer me, please. We need you.

MOTHMA | JOURNAL ENTRY

BAIL WAS OLDER WITH MUCH MORE EXPERIENCE. THOUGH I GREW UP IN A POLITICAL FAMILY, HE WAS HEIR TO A <u>ROYAL DYNASTY</u>. WHEN I ARRIVED ON CORUSCANT FOR MY FIRST LEGISLATIVE SESSION, I SOUGHT OUT BAIL'S COUNSEL, CERTAIN THAT SUCH A DISTINGUISHED PERSONAGE WOULD POSSESS THE WISDOM OF A SAGE.

CONTINUED

MOTHMA | JOURNAL ENTRY

Instead, he told me something shockingly egalitarian, something that put me instantly at ease. "No one here," he said, "or anywhere else, truly knows what they're doing. So if you feel that way, you're in good company."

Of course Bail went on to teach me so much, but his point stayed with me. <u>You have something worth adding even when you think you don't.</u>

Bail and Breha . . . oh fates, Breha is lost too. Leia, their adopted daughter, their legacy. How they treasured her.

I'm numb. Paralyzed. The loss of so many is disorienting. The pain is so great. I know the Alliance must fight, but we must also mourn. I must mourn, and I have no time to do that.

Bail is with the Force now. I'd much prefer he were here with me.

HENDRI UNDERHOLT

Commander, I need your signature on these forms. It can't wait. Commander, NOW.

MOTHMA | JOURNAL ENTRY

Oh, the dressing-down I have given Hendri for overreaching her station. How desperately I needed her to do exactly that.

A leader leads. Looking backwards will not honor Bail or the Alderaan dead. We will honor them by fighting. By facing down Palpatine.

Plans or no, we will . . . must destroy the Death Star.

Sometimes the hard road is the only road. —Leia

CLASSIFIED DOCUMENT—CLEARANCE LEVEL: 

HARINAR/DRAVEN PROG40241

RI 035-X5

TRACKING DEVICE

TO: GENERAL DRAVEN

FROM: MAJOR HARINAR

As suspected, the smuggling freighter *Millennium Falcon* had an Imperial tracking device on board.

SUB RI 035-X5 TRACKING DEVICE

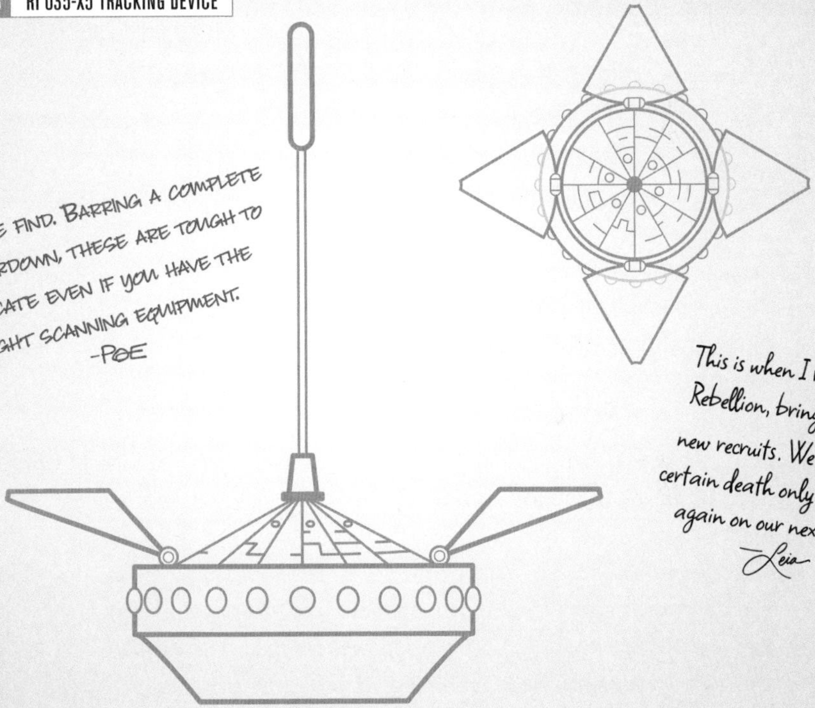

NICE FIND. BARRING A COMPLETE TEARDOWN, THESE ARE TOUGH TO LOCATE EVEN IF YOU HAVE THE RIGHT SCANNING EQUIPMENT.
-POE

This is when I rejoined the Rebellion, bringing a few new recruits. We'd escaped certain death only to face it again on our next stop.
—Leia

It's an IDMR custom job with a hyperwave narrow-band transceiver, which was definitely transmitting when we found it and shut it down.

Guess who's coming to Yavin?

CLASSIFIED DOCUMENT—CLEARANCE LEVEL: 

DODONNA/MOTHMA PROG40288

RI 077-X5

INTEL UPDATE CIC: DEATH STAR PLANS

TO: COMMANDER MOTHMA

FROM: GENERAL DODONNA

Draven confirms that the plans have been transferred out of Princess Leia's astromech droid and into Base One's computer for analysis. I need all eyes on this data. Highest priority.

DOC #49941463-ALL

TO: GEN. DRAVEN, ALLIANCE INTELLIGENCE

FROM: PVT. WEEMS, SIGNALS INTEL TECH

SUBJ: GAP IN THE ARMOR

We've scanned every centimeter of these schematics looking for Dr. Erso's flaw, making sure we're not falling for a decoy or missing the obvious. I hate to share credit, but that little blue R2 unit has been surprisingly helpful.

To sum up:

- The weakness in the connection between the primary power amplifier and the hypermatter reactor can be exploited by a high-energy rupture.
- The Death Star's exhaust ports vent superheated gases from the hypermatter reactor to prevent it from overheating.
- One secondary exhaust port is particularly vulnerable. It's at the end of a meridian trench guarded by turbolaser batteries.

This is it, this is our target. What do we have that could rip this vulnerability wide open? A proton torpedo could do it. (Energy weapons aren't enough and the zone is ray shielded anyway.) Making the shot that starts the chain reaction, though—that's the tricky part. The exhaust port aperture is less than two meters wide.

TRICKY IS AN UNDERSTATEMENT. AT THOSE SPEEDS, UNDER FIRE, WHILE BEING CHASED? I COULD DO IT, BUT IT'S STILL A TOUGH SHOT. -POE

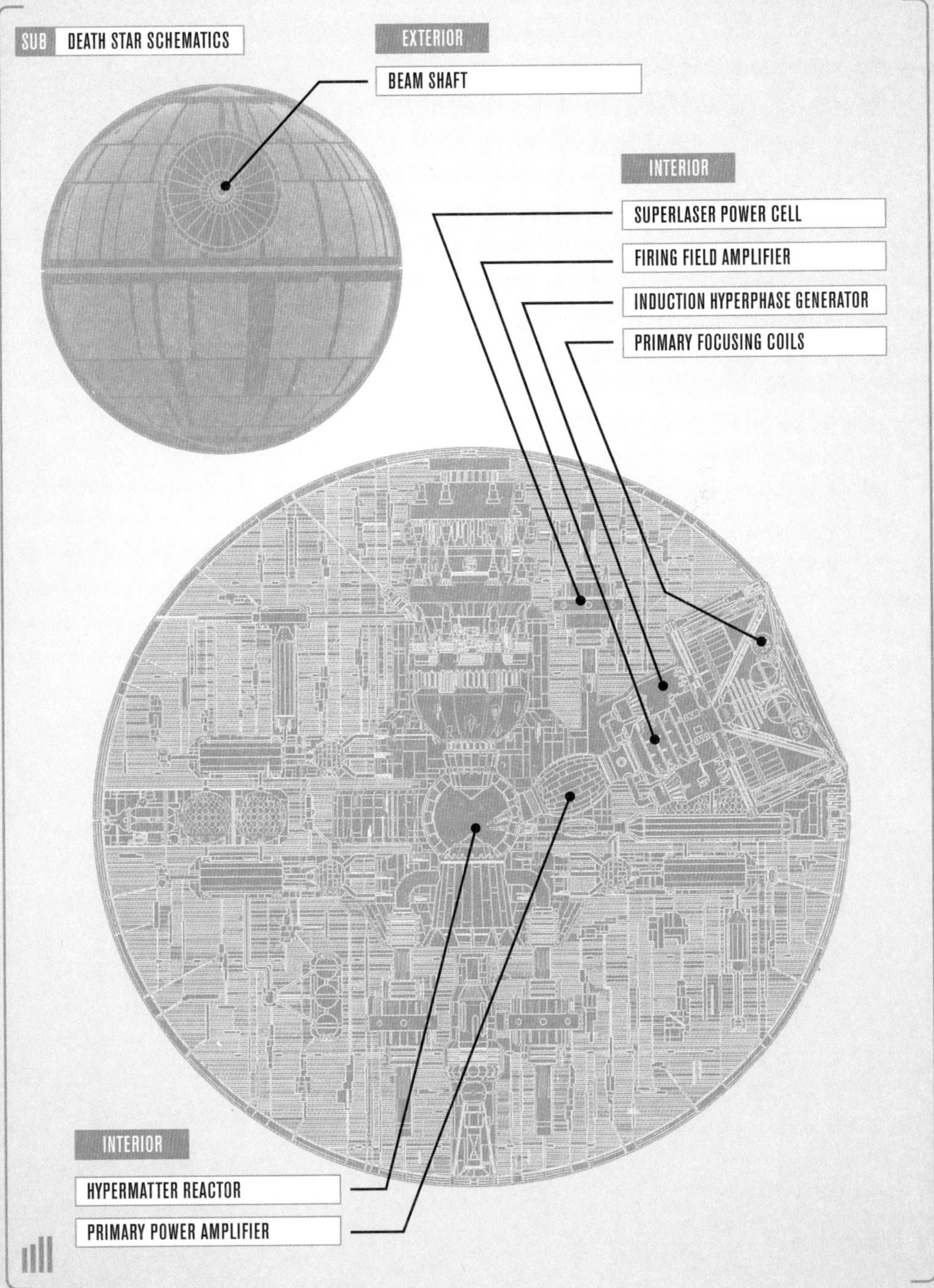
SUB DEATH STAR SCHEMATICS
EXTERIOR
BEAM SHAFT
INTERIOR
SUPERLASER POWER CELL
FIRING FIELD AMPLIFIER
INDUCTION HYPERPHASE GENERATOR
PRIMARY FOCUSING COILS
INTERIOR
HYPERMATTER REACTOR
PRIMARY POWER AMPLIFIER

TO: ALL COMMAND STAFF
FROM: GEN. DODONNA, SECTOR COMMAND
SUBJ: PLANNING THE ATTACK

You've read Weems' report. Let's discuss options.

According to the schematics, the Death Star has ten thousand turbolasers. Fortunately, they're spaced out across a surface area of more than 45,000 square kilometers. It's a loose defense designed to repel a large-scale fleet assault.

Given the loss of the *Profundity* at Scarif, we don't have much of a fleet left. This could ironically be a blessing. Our starfighters could make it through the Death Star's turbolaser screen. I've spoken to Squadron leader Vander, who is confident his Gold Squadron pilots can make the torpedo shot in their Y-wings.

I recommend deploying the Y-wings as bombers, after calibrating their targeting computers for fast approach and precision release. X-wings will serve in an escort role.

Even if it didn't have any guns at all, a fleet would have a hard time doing more than pockmark damage to a battlemoon of that size. Admiral Ackbar

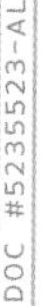

TO: MON MOTHMA
FROM: GEN. DRAVEN, ALLIANCE INTELLIGENCE
SUBJ: DETERMINING THE VERACITY OF OUR INTEL

Commander, I'm forwarding this so that you're aware of the debate. This does not change my recommendation that we act immediately. The stakes are simply too high.

COL. DELTO: No, what I'm saying is that it's too easy. One single flaw that brings down the entire battle station in a nanosecond?

MAJ. HARINAR: And your point is?

CONTINUED

DOC #5235523-ALL

OFFICIAL DOCUMENT

COL. DELTO: My point is, it has to be bait. The Empire is using this supposed flaw to lure us into a trap.

MAJ. HARINAR: If that were true, don't you think they'd make the flaw something subtler? The fact that it's so catastrophic is exactly the sort of cascading oversight that crops up all the time. Imperial Intelligence wouldn't be that blatant.

COL. DELTO: Aha, but you see that's just it. The Empire knows that we know that they wouldn't be so blatant, so they do exactly that. To confound our expectations.

MAJ. HARINAR: Hmm. But the fact that we're discussing it as a possibility in this room right now is evidence that we *know* that they know that we know that they wouldn't be so blatant. Ergo, the Death Star's flaw is plausible.

COL. DELTO: Yes, but consider this: if they *know* that we know that they know that we know—

GEN. DRAVEN: Gentlemen, let's wrap this up.

END DOCUMENT

MON MOTHMA

Hendri, you will be accompanying me to the fleet rendezvous. We leave in an hour. Bring the data cache.

HENDRI UNDERHOLT

We're evacuating Yavin 4?

MON MOTHMA

No. We're fighting. But if we lose at Yavin, the Alliance will keep fighting.

MON MOTHMA

I can't do anything more here. Very soon we will celebrate or we will mourn. But neither outcome absolves us of our duty. With Ackbar's help I can prepare fleet contingencies and counterattacks should things turn out for the worst.

After the squadrons launched, I stared at the sky until the specks vanished. I couldn't blame Han for running, but a part of me could already feel our reunion. —Leia

PARTIAL TRANSCRIPT OF WAR ROOM RECORDINGS: BASE ONE, YAVIN 4

Control Officer: Sensors indicate the Death Star has exited hyperspace on the far side of the gas giant. Currently moving around the planet for a clear shot at Yavin 4.

CONTINUED

GENERAL DODONNA: Calculate their orbital speed. Are there any other reversion signatures?

GENERAL WILLARD: Negative. Just the one.

PRINCESS LEIA ORGANA: That's a blessing. No Star Destroyers in support.

CONTROL OFFICER: At its current rate, estimated time to Death Star firing range is fifteen minutes.

COLONEL COR: Red and Gold Squadrons are en route and should be nearing visual range. Pilot comms have been patched in.

GENERAL DODONNA: Squad leaders, execute attack pattern Alpha.

CONTROL OFFICER: Red Six destroyed.

GENERAL DODONNA: The longer we're up there, the more we'll lose to attrition. Where's that bombing run?

CONTROL OFFICER: Red Four destroyed.

PRINCESS LEIA ORGANA: Tell him to get out of there.

GENERAL DODONNA: They're not going to make it in time.

CONTROL OFFICER: Death Star will be in range in one minute.

GENERAL DODONNA: Red Five, this is Base One. You're cleared for your run.

CONTROL OFFICER: General! Confirming reactor surge!

GENERAL DODONNA: All rebel craft, this is Base One. Withdraw to safe blast range immediately. Repeat, withdraw to safe blast range immediately.

TO: The free peoples of the galaxy
FROM: Mon Mothma of the Rebel Alliance

Though you live under the Empire, no tyrant can lay claim to your free will.

The Rebel Alliance captured top-secret information concerning an Imperial battle station able to obliterate planets, and subsequently destroyed the superweapon near the Outer Rim planet of Yavin. This Death Star was responsible for wiping out the Holy City of Jedha and annihilating the beloved Core World of Alderaan.

Imperial propagandists claimed that a mining accident brought down the Holy City. They will no doubt twist the Alderaan tragedy to their cynical benefit.

You deserve to know the truth. The Empire murdered billions, using a weapon so indiscriminate in its effect that its very existence is a crime. The Rebel Alliance removed that weapon, saving billions from the Emperor's wrath.

Act now, while the Empire is reeling. Act now, because Imperial invincibility has been exposed as a lie and a fantasy.

Join us and press the advantage against our enemy. The Rebel Alliance is committed to restoring the ideals of the Republic and giving a voice to the people. In our ranks you are valued. Join us and fight.

I remember this moment and this speech. No more Senate, no more secret weapons. The combatants had revealed themselves, and the battle line burned bright and clear. —Leia

SHELL TOP-LEVEL/CATEGORY

ALLIANCE CHRON 3

ABSTRACT:

Regrouping

Hendri Underholt

ARCHIVIST

STANDARD DATE: 19–22 AFE

(AFTER THE FORMATION OF THE EMPIRE)

MOTHMA | JOURNAL ENTRY

We've done it. We've done it twice now, in rapid succession and against forces we had little chance of besting. Do the victories at Scarif and Yavin legitimize our movement? Or am I desperately trying to rationalize our successes?

We blocked the Empire from achieving omnipotence, yet we barely scratched its armory. When our jubilation wears off, we will again face the same grim numbers.

The Empire has the machinery, the muscle, and the might. They won't underestimate us again. The Alliance has to disappear, and quickly.

With the company I keep, voices are constantly urging me to credit positive outcomes to luck or the Force. I prefer to claim the credit for actions of my own making. —Leia

DOC #5422521-ALL

FROM: MON MOTHMA
TO: TYNNRA PAMLO
SUBJ: TELLING THE YAVIN STORY

Tynnra, you have my approval. Let us capitalize on the persuasive power of this victory. All of the following assets are at your disposal:

- Long-range telemetry recordings of the Death Star's destruction (Col. Delto will issue limited decryptions at your request)
- In-flight footage captured by Gold and Red Squadron (Delto)
- Holographic footage captured at medal ceremony (route all permissions through Olia Choko in communications)
- Text of official statements: Mon Mothma, Admiral Ackbar, Leia Organa
- Various graphical compositions and reproducible iconography (see attachment 00RAY2//WREN)

Please work with Hendri Underholt in my office to coordinate your efforts. Thank you.

THE REBELLION IS
TRIUMPHANT.

THE EMPIRE IS
IN RETREAT.

JOIN THE ALLIANCE

TO RESTORE THE REPUBLIC.

I have my complaints with the way the New Republic dismisses our fight, but it's better than receiving a public branding as political criminals.

–Holdo

TRINEBULON NEWS

The Truth, Straight from the Source

REBEL SNEAK ATTACK KILLS THOUSANDS

Gordian Reach, Outer Rim Territories—Proving that no crime is too vile for traitors, rebel saboteurs killed thousands of Imperial soldiers in a cowardly attack on an orbital station.

The raid occurred near Yavin in the Gordian Reach, where top rebel leaders had fled to escape the Empire's Outer Rim peacekeeping campaign. Using a combination of treachery and subterfuge, rebel agents ignited the station's reactor and triggered a catastrophic explosion.

Immediately after the tragedy, rebel propagandists released images that showed the perpetrators of the attack smiling and laughing as Leia Organa, former Senator of Alderaan, handed out glittering medals.

(continued on p. 2)

CYNABAR'S INFONET

Always Bet on the Big CYN

THIS WAS THE FIRST TIME WE WON THE USE OF THE UNCHARTED HYPERSPACE BACK LANES.

– EMATT

REBELLION ON THE UPSWING? NOT SO FAST

Nal Hutta—As reported in Nal Hutta Kal'tamok, the Hutt Council issued an earnings announcement today that contained a peripheral acknowledgment of the Rebel Alliance's victory at Yavin. It might not seem like much, but the move is a huge step toward diplomatic legitimization of the Rebellion—and it's already casting a chill over Imperial/Hutt relations.

It should be clear the Hutts are betting on future profits from doing business with the Rebellion, which means that Mon Mothma's movement stands a better-than-average chance of sticking around for at least a few more cycles.

Our analysts at Cynabar's tackled the same problem and came to a more pessimistic conclusion. Don't start waving Alliance flags just yet—the rebels are in real trouble. They're leaning on unreliable credit flows and supply chains, their military isn't worth much, and their coalition is shakier than it seems.

IF YOU'RE A BOUNTY HUNTER: The guild still hasn't issued an official policy on accepting rebel jobs. Independent hunters willing to take their chances should work with third-party bounty brokers only.

IF YOU'RE A SMUGGLER: Don't get conned—your odds of getting paid by the rebels are lower than your chance of getting boarded by Imperial customs. No matter how much they're promising. Protect your livelihood.

Terrible lanes! Unswept! Ships would come out the other end pelted with micrometeoroids that had been swept up in hyperswirl!

Admiral Ackbar

DOC #5523332-ALL

TO: COMMANDER MON MOTHMA

FROM: GENERAL DODONNA

SUBJ: PRINCESS LEIA ORGANA

General Draven just informed me that the Empire placed a 10 million credit bounty on the head of Princess Leia Organa. We made her a symbol when we released those medal ceremony images. I am recommending that the princess remain here at Base One under protective guard until we can guarantee her safe passage to the Alliance flagship.

DOC #5656672-ALL

TO: GENERAL DODONNA

FROM: COMMANDER MON MOTHMA

SUBJ: PRINCESS LEIA ORGANA

I heard what just happened. I know what you're going to ask.

Leia broke the quarantine you imposed and she commandeered your personal shuttle. Her pilot, Lt. Verlaine, outflew two of our best starfighter aces before jumping to hyperspace.

So what should we do about it? Nothing.

Leia and Lt. Verlaine are Alderaanians. They've gone to seek out other refugees of Alderaan. Survivors rallying other survivors. It's a potent symbol and a moral duty. Instead of holding her back, let us see where she will take us.

HENDRI UNDERHOLT

Commander, Admiral Ackbar is sending practically every ship to Yavin to assist with the evacuation of Base One. You can stay here aboard the *Esperance*, but it's not leaving until tomorrow at the earliest.

MON MOTHMA

Which ship is the next to depart?

HENDRI UNDERHOLT

The *Nangilima*. It's jumping to Yavin in less than an hour.

MON MOTHMA

Grab your things and meet me on board. We have heroes to congratulate.

CLASSIFIED DOCUMENT—CLEARANCE LEVEL: 

ACKBAR/MOTHMA PROG40852

RI 075-N1

YAVIN'S DEFENSE

TO: COMMANDER MOTHMA

FROM: ADMIRAL ACKBAR

Commander— It is impossible to know when the Empire will strike at Yavin. Retaliation is inevitable, yet they may leave us be and seize the sectors I have just now left unprotected.

Our gravest threat at Yavin would be an armada supporting a gravity-roiling *Interdictor* cruiser. Such a formation would prevent our ships from jumping to hyperspace and leave us vulnerable to tractor beam immobilization and turbolaser crossfire. I've deployed our warships to counter this scenario.

Though the *Profundity*'s loss is keenly felt, the fight goes on. Rest assured that *Home One* is more than equipped to fill the role of Alliance flagship.

A wise assessment from my younger self. The Empire did indeed grab muc of the Overic Griplink at my expense.
Admiral Ackbar

ADDENDUM: LT. SESFAN

See supplementary report from the Mon Cal shipyards at Telaris concerning warship conversion and anticipated launch schedules.

DOC #5235523-ALL

TO: COL. COR, STARFIGHTER COMMAND

FROM: LT. ANTILLES (RED 2)

SUBJ: PATROL REPORT: YAVIN PERIMETER

After clearing orbit, Patrol X-wing (Snoop 2), equipped with Fabritech high-gain recon sensor package, made a full perimeter circuit to scan for signs of Imperial incursion or passive observation devices.

SMART STUFF. PACKING THE RECON GEAR INTO AN X-WING BEATS A DEDICATED RECON CRAFT EVERY TIME.
-POE

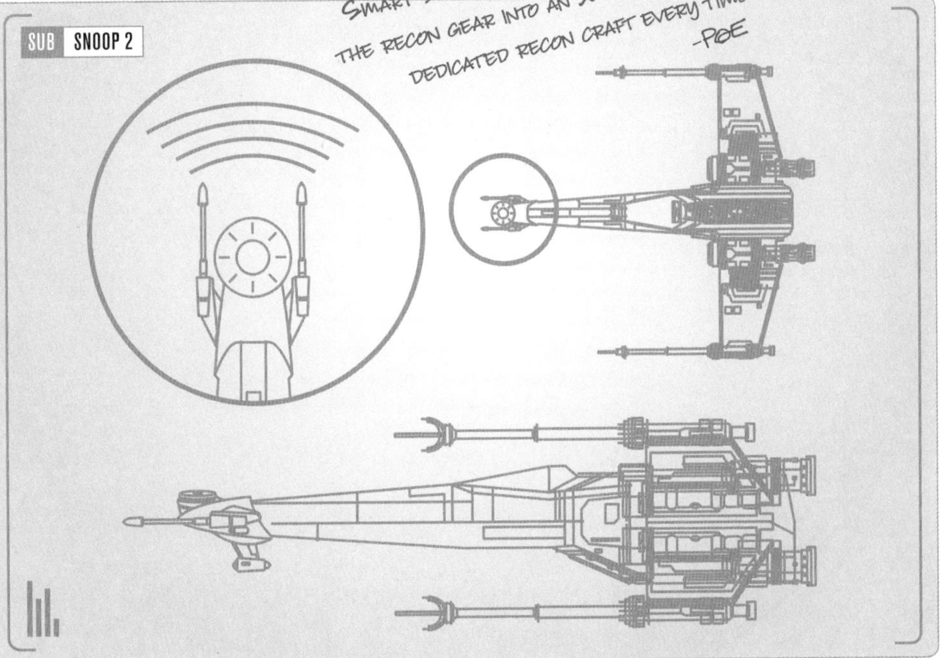

SUB SNOOP 2

Sweep One: Far side of Yavin's sensor shadow
This segment received added attention in light of yesterday's unconfirmed sightings of an Imperial scout ship in the vicinity (or at least a sensor contact matching the profile of same). Sweep came up negative for foreign objects or signals.

Sweep Two: Near spinward arc
Negative for foreign objects or signals.

CONTINUED

DOC #5235523-ALL

Sweep Three: Far spinward arc
Had a bit of a scare when a long-range threat popped up that matched the profile of an Imperial probe droid.

By the time I reached the halfway point my sensors assembled a more accurate model: a metal-rich asteroid three meters in diameter. Turns out its mirrored facets had bounced my own pings back at me, which tricked the sensors into thinking an inert rock might be a powered-up hunter killer. False alarm.

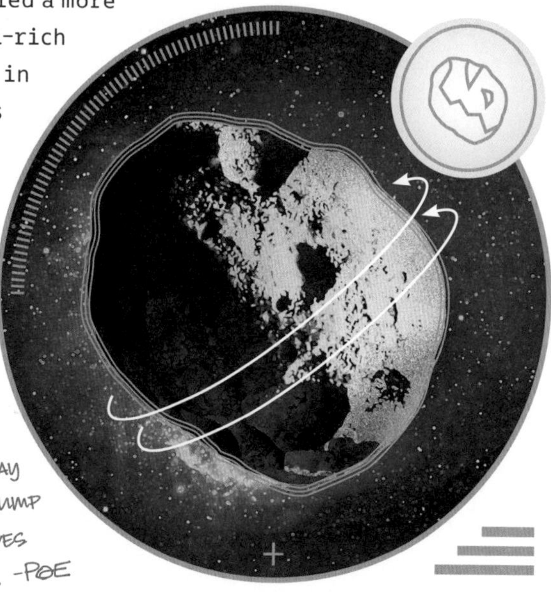

I'VE HEARD OF THIS HAPPENING. ANOTHER WAY TO MESS WITH PERIMETER PATROLS IS TO DUMP A CARGO OF TINY SENSOR SCREAMERS. DRIVES THE ENEMY CRAZY CHECKING OUT EACH ONE. -POE

END DOCUMENT

TO: ALL ALLIANCE INTEL HEADS
FROM: GENERAL CRACKEN
SUBJ: IMMINENT THREAT

OFFICIAL DOCUMENT

We have multiple confirmations. Due to the Death Star's destruction and the resulting command structure shakeup, Imperial Intelligence has decided it's better to strike now before everyone gets reassigned.

All senior commanders in Imperial Intelligence and the Imperial Security Bureau have been authorized to move against their current targets at once. This is going to get messy.

RI 052-IN2

HIGH-VALUE EXTRACTION: SHRIKES

TO: COMMANDER MOTHMA

FROM: GENERAL DRAVEN

Commander– You've seen the report from Taanab. The Shrikes—one of our recon units assigned to scout for a new headquarters base—was wiped out in a shootout with agents of the Imperial Security Bureau.

Early data indicated no survivors, but Pvt. Weems just captured a burst transmission from Hutt Space. The sender has been identified as Lt. Caluan Ematt, the Shrikes' leader. Ematt escaped to Cyrkon and is in urgent need of extraction.

The ISB is closing in on his position and Cyrkon is crawling with money-hungry fringers who'd give him up for a quarter credit. Before Scarif, Capt. Andor would have been my first choice for a mission like this. Now I'm scrambling to find someone with underworld familiarity and expertise with the Hutts. Expect my recommendation shortly.

I DIDN'T EXPECT TO FIND THIS HERE. THE DAYS AFTER THE TAANAB AMBUSH WERE SOME OF THE WORST OF MY LIFE. – EMATT

COMMANDER MOTHMA TO GENERAL DRAVEN

General, I have two recruits who are exactly what you're looking for.

GENERAL DRAVEN TO COMMANDER MOTHMA

You're not thinking of a certain Corellian and Wookiee, are you? They're untrained, undisciplined, and they don't know how to take orders.

COMMANDER MOTHMA TO GENERAL DRAVEN

As I recall, Jyn Erso worked out rather well? Keep me updated.

SOLO AND CHEWBACCA NEVER HAVE TO BUY A DRINK WHEN I'M AROUND. I MISS THOSE TWO MANIACS. I OWE THEM SO MUCH. - EMATT

CLASSIFIED DOCUMENT—CLEARANCE LEVEL:

DRAVEN/ONORAN PROG41022

RI 057-IN2

MISSION PLAN: ASSAULT ON CYMOON

TO: GENERAL ONORAN

FROM: GENERAL DRAVEN

Losing the Death Star cost the Empire more than just a superweapon. If the Death Star was even half full, it cost them hundreds of AT-ATs and thousands of assault shuttles and TIE fighters. To close that gap, the Empire is going to ramp up production. We cannot let them.

TARGET: CYMOON 1

Of the major Imperial weapons plants, I recommend Factory Alpha on Cymoon 1 in the Corellian Industrial Cluster.

It's known as the largest weapons factory in the galaxy with plants operated by Imperial contractors KDY, Sienar, Lor-

CONTINUED

onar, and Blastech. It is also in the heart of Imperial space and thus relatively underdefended.

MISSION SUMMARY

Infiltration, sabotage, and rapid exfiltration using Imperial/Hutt supply chains as cover

COMMAND PERSONNEL

- Princess Leia Organa: Squad leader
- Lt. Luke Skywalker: Squad pilot
- Han Solo: Squad infiltrator (strong underworld connections; demonstrated better-than-expected performance on Cyrkon Extraction [ref. DD-1575])

MISSION OVERVIEW

- Stage 1: Intercept Hutt shuttle above Tatooine and capture craft. Target shuttle will be carrying Jabba's industrial emissary (Anchorhead Tac-Comm to provide transponder ID and final flight schedule).
- Stage 2: Land shuttle at Cymoon 1 and meet with Imperial overseer. Solo will pose as Hutt emissary with Organa and Skywalker as bodyguards.
- Stage 3: Sabotage of Globus-X9 power core should flatten Factory Alpha. Should opportunity arise, squad will free captives and/or seize Imperial records and experimental tech.
- Stage 4: Escape via Hutt shuttle. Backup options:
    - Imperial cargo shuttles
    - Imperial gunships coming off assembly line

END DOCUMENT

A bold move, striking the Corellian Industrial Cluster at this point in the war. After demilitarization, it never regained the manufacturing heights it enjoyed under the Empire. -Statura

DOC #5677665-ALL

TO: MON MOTHMA

FROM: LEIA ORGANA

SUBJ: ARRTH-ENO MISSION

As payback for our recent successes at Cymoon and elsewhere, Palpatine has announced plans to execute all political prisoners incarcerated at Arrth-Eno. Attached is a summary of the mission I've been planning with Intelligence.

We know them. These are our colleagues, our friends. Most senators didn't escape underground like us. They were blindsided by the news of the Senate's dissolution and opened their doors to find ISB loyalty officers waiting to put them in shackles.

At the recommendation of General Draven, we're activating one of our Coruscant deep-cover agents (Eneb Ray, operating as Tharius Demo) to extract them before the deadline. We won't be able to use him again but the payoff is worth it.

Shea, Tanner, Nadea, Ivor . . . we'll see them all soon.

So hopeful. I thought I'd been given the chance to save them because I couldn't save Alderaan. I couldn't accept it at the time, but this failure - this personal failure - broke an emotional dam..

—Leia

DOC #5677535-ALL

TO: COMMANDER MOTHMA

FROM: GENERAL DRAVEN

SUBJ: ARRTH-ENO FAILURE

Prison extraction failed. Total loss of life.

Orbital imagery indicates the facility was leveled. I have reason to believe our agent on the inside deviated from the plan based on news that the Emperor might visit Arrth-Eno in person. The temptation to eliminate Palpatine may have compromised the plan.

CLASSIFIED DOCUMENT—CLEARANCE LEVEL: 

CRACKEN/MOTHMA PROG41089

RI 011-N2

TAGGE OFFENSIVE

TO: COMMANDER MOTHMA

FROM: GENERAL CRACKEN

It seems Cassio Tagge has been promoted to the rank of grand general. He's essentially the new Tarkin, and, save the Emperor, is currently our biggest threat. Like Tarkin his focus is on bullying the Outer Rim into submission.

Not a naval commander, but despite that failing Tagge proved to be a canny adversary. —Admiral Ackbar

Some of his tactics are taught at naval academies today. Tagge excelled at data collection and analysis. -Statura

MON MOTHMA TO GENERAL CRACKEN

Thank you, Airen. I'm familiar with Tagge, and anyone who travels among Coruscant elites is well acquainted with his family. Tell me what you think he's going to do next.

GENERAL CRACKEN TO MON MOTHMA

Tagge's base of operations is the SSD *Annihilator* (see Ackbar's naval report for more). He's a cautious, thoughtful commander.

If I had to guess, I'd say he is going to shore up support among the underworld before he attacks us directly. With the Mining Guild and the Hutt Council reasonably obedient, I'd peg his next target to be Black Sun or Crymorah. Such a move would cause significant splashback for our own operations as we share the Rim's uncharted back lanes with these syndicates.

The Empire's raids against the underworld had far-reaching effects, driving many syndicates to sign pacts with the Alliance. Even today the Resistance relies on those ties.—Statura

MON MOTHMA TO GENERAL CRACKEN

Yes. For now, I feel we must view an Imperial campaign against the underworld as our problem too. But only for now. When we win this war, we can afford to be choosier in picking our partners.

CLASSIFIED DOCUMENT—CLEARANCE LEVEL: 

ACKBAR/MOTHMA PROG41097

RI 043-N1

EXECUTOR-CLASS STAR DREADNOUGHT

TO: COMMANDER MOTHMA

FROM: ADMIRAL ACKBAR

I denounced the first of these vessels, you'll recall, as Palpatine's folly in excess. Yet despite the accuracy of my

CONTINUED

ACKBAR/MOTHMA PROG41097

insight, I somehow failed to anticipate that he would still hunger for more.

The Empire has the capacity to build them, of course. If only the Alliance could control such resources . . .

These dreadnoughts, or Super Star Destroyers, are more akin to mobile command centers than proper warships, yet they can annihilate an armada through concentrated arms alone. Five thousand turbolasers . . . what could withstand such a broadside?

KDY records indicate the class was named for the *Executor*, though complications at the Kuat yards have delayed its launch. Following are the Empire's most critical SSDs, both those currently in service and those still under construction:

- *Executor*
- *Annihilator* (assigned to Grand General Tagge)
- *Arbitrator*
- *Ravager*
- *Eclipse* (rumored to be the flagship of Emperor Palpatine)

The Annihilator fell victim to pirates, and New Republic forces chased the Arbitrator into a black hole. -Statura

After Endor, the New Republic captured three Super Star Destroyers. The Ravager, I believe, ended up in the hands of Grand Admiral Rae Sloane. -Holdo

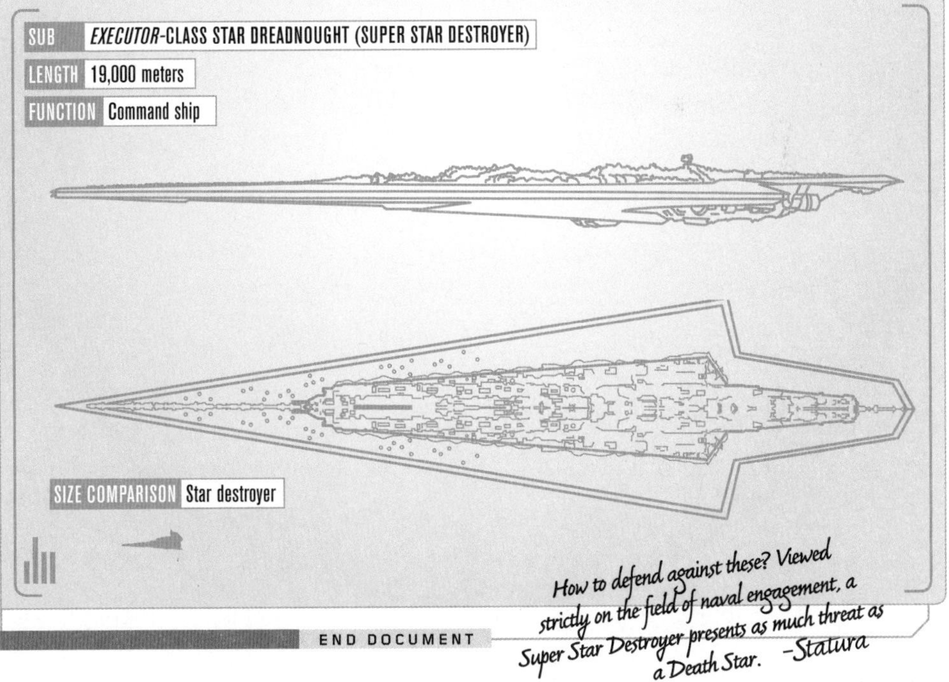

How to defend against these? Viewed strictly on the field of naval engagement, a Super Star Destroyer presents as much threat as a Death Star. -Statura

END DOCUMENT

CYNABAR'S INFONET

Always Bet on the Big CYN

Watch Your Backs: Imperial Aggression Is Real

What's with the surge in Imperial raids against the underworld? Maybe losing a Death Star embarrassed the Emperor enough to seek easy wins against players who don't even want to fight.

Let's start with the trade deal that Jabba struck with Lord Vader, which was signed under duress according to our insiders. Consider also the territorial restrictions imposed on Black Sun and the mandatory tithing levied against the Rodian Junk Cartel.

Thanks to Grand General Tagge, the still-warm corpses of the Crymorah cartel and Son-tuul Pride are the latest casualties in this undeclared war.

Readers of Cynabar's InfoNet should regard the unfolding crisis with sober eyes. Our analysts have prepared region-by-region recommendations. Each can be accessed for a small fee.

OFFICIAL REPORT

NAVAL LOSSES: RECLUSE'S NEBULA

ATTN: Commander Mothma

REPORT FILED BY: General Baccam Grafis, Ordnance & Supply

The skirmish in the Recluse's Nebula resulted in a NET LOSS to the Alliance's naval assets. Should the Alliance continue on its current course, we will exhaust our fleet elements within eighteen months (with a margin of error of plus or minus three months).

Following is my department's accounting of the Recluse engagement and the associated adjustments.

Losses

- One BTL Y-wing: 130,000 credits
- One *Lambda*-class T-4a shuttle, used: 180,000 credits
- One *Alpha*-class Xg-1 Star Wing: 125,000 credits
- Three cargo containers, empty: 90,000 credits
- One cargo container, full (grain): 75,000 credits

(continued on p. 2)

CYNABAR'S INFONET

Always Bet on the Big CYN

Grakkus' Games Go Too Far

Nar Shaddaa—Most indie operators know all about the gladiator matches that Grakkus the Hutt hosts. Of course, this ignores the bantha in the ballroom, namely that Imperial law outlaws gladiatorial combat.

That technicality bit Grakkus hard yesterday when a gladiator match escalated into an all-out brawl between rebels, stormtroopers, and the pro fighters and IG MagnaGuards employed by Grakkus. The debacle ended when the rebels fled and the Imps arrested everybody who was left.

"This never would have happened if the rebels hadn't turned a sporting event into a political affair," complained FwittsinPru, Troig spokesbeing for the Obroan Oddsmakers. "Some things aren't appropriate venues for 'freedom this' or 'equality that.' The Rebel Alliance needs to grow up."

(continued on p. 2)

Commander—Message just received from Commander Narra at our starfighter base on Vrogas Vas. We're already formulating an attack plan. —Dodonna

VADER DOWN.

I REPEAT, DARTH VADER HAS BEEN SHOT DOWN ON VROGAS VAS.

THIS IS RED LEADER CALLING FOR ASSISTANCE FROM ALL AVAILABLE ALLIANCE FORCES.

DOC #5722811-ALL

TO: ALLIANCE COMMAND STAFF

FROM: MON MOTHMA

SUBJ: VADER ON VROGAS VAS

I am approving Princess Leia's request for a coordinated Alliance strike. Lord Darth Vader is alone and unprotected on Vrogas Vas. Capture is preferred; elimination is acceptable. Let's get this monster.

CLASSIFIED DOCUMENT—CLEARANCE LEVEL: 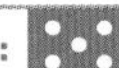

NARRA/DODONNA PROG41209

RI 070-X4

ACTION AT VROGAS VAS

TO: GENERAL DODONNA

FROM: COMMANDER NARRA (RED LEADER)

I'VE READ THE REPORTS ON THIS. NO PILOT SHOULD EVER BE AS SKILLED AS VADER WAS HERE—NOT EVEN ME. MAYBE THE FORCE IS GOOD FOR SOMETHING AFTER ALL.
- POE

General, looking back at the Vrogas Vas engagement, there isn't much for the Alliance to count in its favor.

To review:

- Darth Vader escaped capture.
- We abandoned our starfighter outpost following the arrival of the Imperial fleet.
- We lost Blue, Gray, and Yellow Squadrons—almost entirely due to Vader's actions as a sole combatant.

On the positive:

- All Alliance command staff members escaped.
- All sensitive information stored at our Vrogas Vas outpost was recovered or intentionally destroyed.
- We captured one high-value prisoner: Dr. Chelli Lona Aphra, remanded to our max security penitentiary at Sunspot.

Despite the wins, we lost this fight. This was one of the worst cullings of starfighter pilots I've ever seen.

MOTHMA | JOURNAL ENTRY

I never wanted to build a military machine, yet here I am overseeing its progress. Deadly force and the urgency of war. This is exactly how Palpatine achieved dictatorship, and he is not a model I wish to emulate.

I am not naïve. Now is not the time for disarmament. Honorable warriors like Ackbar, Rieekan, and Dodonna will pursue specific objectives and stand down when those objectives are won. I trust them.

Trust, however, is not a governing philosophy. When our victory finally arrives, we cannot maintain a centralized military. A coalition of planetary or sector militaries, perhaps—something that breaks the link between political power and military control. If we don't do it, we'll only foster rebellion from within.

After Endor, this is exactly what happened. —Holdo

And now we lack the strength to fight back against the First Order. —Leia

CLASSIFIED DOCUMENT—CLEARANCE LEVEL:

RIEEKAN/MOTHMA PROG41219

RI 099-X1
MID RIM OFFENSIVE
TO: COMMANDER MOTHMA
FROM: GENERAL RIEEKAN

With the Empire still in a relative state of disorganization, now is the best time for us to mobilize the Alliance's ground forces. We can't continue to strike and immediately retreat. We need to capture actual planets, and hold our territory against counterattack.

CONTINUED

RIEEKAN/MOTHMA PROG41219

A tall order in light of the Empire's numerical superiority, but we can make inroads by picking our battles.

I recommend launching several attacks in the Mid Rim. The Empire has the Core on lockdown, and the Outer Rim is overprotected as the Empire tries to roust us from our hiding spots. By contrast, the Mid Rim offers numerous advantages. We currently enjoy much sympathy in the Mid Rim.

You will soon receive a detailed battle plan for what we are calling the Mid Rim Offensive. With your approval, we will start taking the galaxy back from Palpatine one planet at a time.

I FOUND MYSELF ON THE VANGUARD OF THE MID OFFENSIVE, ON ORD TIDDELL AND ELSEWHE WE TRIED TO GRAB TOO MUCH, TOO FAST. – EMAT

END DOCUMENT

DOC #5973872-ALL

TO: MON MOTHMA
FROM: GENERAL ONORAN
SUBJ: GENERAL MADINE

Commander, I'm forwarding the following in response to the debacle on the Ghost Moon. Gen. Madine has reason to believe that the extermination of our soldiers occurred at the hands of Imperial SCAR troopers.

I know you've been hesitant to embrace an ex-Imperial like Madine, but we'll only hurt ourselves if we marginalize defectors.

CLASSIFIED DOCUMENT—CLEARANCE LEVEL: 

MADINE/ONORAN PROG45501

RI 166-X4
SCAR TROOPERS
TO: GENERAL ONORAN
FROM: GENERAL MADINE

Regarding elite stormtrooper squads, I can confirm that they're more than rumors. For years, Imperial regiments have been known for lockstep obedience, but we can't count on that predictability much longer.

CONTINUED

The Stormtrooper Corps is getting smarter. Take a look at Inferno Squad, an Imperial Navy unit made up of the best of the best. They eliminated the remnants of Saw Gerrera's Partisans.

Before I left Imperial SpecForces, I was privy to briefings with operational relevance. I can verify that the SCAR program matches the reports that you've seen coming in from your Rim engagements.

We shouldn't have been surprised. It's the same model the Republic used for Clone Force 99, an unorthodox unit known as the "Bad Batch."
—Holdo

SCAR: Special Commando Advanced Recon Trooper

Elite stormtroopers who are afforded an unusual degree of autonomy. They are deployed in small squads led by a sergeant.

One such unit, Task Force 99, is attached to an elite legion answering to the highest echelons of Imperial command. I am certain more units exist.

I have taken the sketches made by the survivor of the Primtara incident and added some notes concerning squad composition.

A. Engineer: Repairs equipment, hotwires transports, boosts comm signals

B. Close-quarters combatant: Experts in vibroblades, electrostaffs, martial arts

C. Slicer: Cracks computer security to steal info or take control of equipment

D. Sniper: Performs battlefield recon and precision attacks from long range

E. Heavy weapons: Hauls the powerful stuff: grenade launcher, repeating blaster cannon, flamethrower

F. Explosives: Carries detonators and mines, and has engineering training to exploit structural weaknesses

CONTINUED

SCAR units will only become more common as the Empire takes its cues from our own successes. Another reason why we must end this war quickly.

CONTINUED

CLASSIFIED DOCUMENT—CLEARANCE LEVEL: 

BALLISTICS REPORT

Alliance Intelligence, Col. Haxen Delto

Lab No.: 0438-370974

Lab Case No.: 7043316172

Victim(s): Rebel soldiers on Primtara outpost

Result(s): Analysis confirms a high-powered blaster repeater was used in the deaths of two rebel troopers found at the site. At least fifteen shots (exhibits A–H) came from this weapon. No energy-cell casings were found in the vicinity.

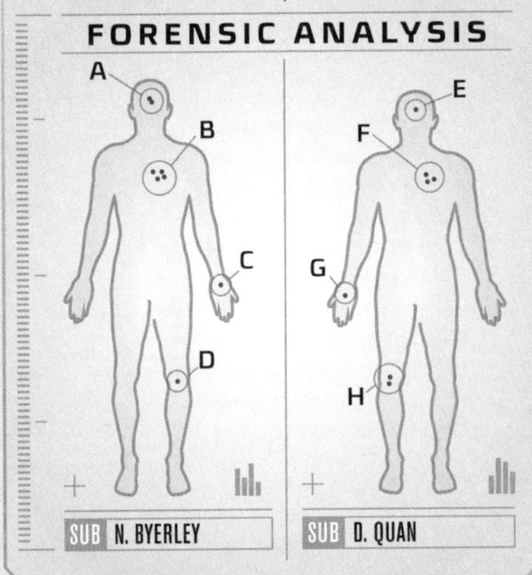

Site underwent spectrographic analysis and chemical processing for trace residues. Due to the absence of a similar weapon for testing, the conclusions contained herein cannot be independently verified and must be viewed with an appropriate degree of scientific reserve. Ballistics testing and report carried out by Lt. Finnilus, Alliance Intelligence

Notes: Front-line stormtroopers do not carry weapons of this caliber. Furthermore, the lack of blaster marks in the walls and floor indicate a proficiency in marksmanship incompatible with stormtrooper performance scores.

These factors would seem to implicate a bounty hunter or mercenary, if we didn't have independent corroboration of stormtrooper presence on Primtara.

END DOCUMENT

CLASSIFIED DOCUMENT—CLEARANCE LEVEL:

RI 022-N1

HARBINGER MISSION

TO: COMMANDER MOTHMA

FROM: GENERAL MADINE

Commander, I realize your attention may be focused on breaking the Tureen blockade, but we have been presented with an opportunity that may not occur again.

The Star Destroyer *Harbinger* is at drydock and vulnerable to a boarding party. With the right team, the Alliance could hijack this vessel and bolster our navy with its first-ever ISD. See attached for mission specifications. Following are the technical schematics of the *Harbinger*.

SUB *HARBINGER*

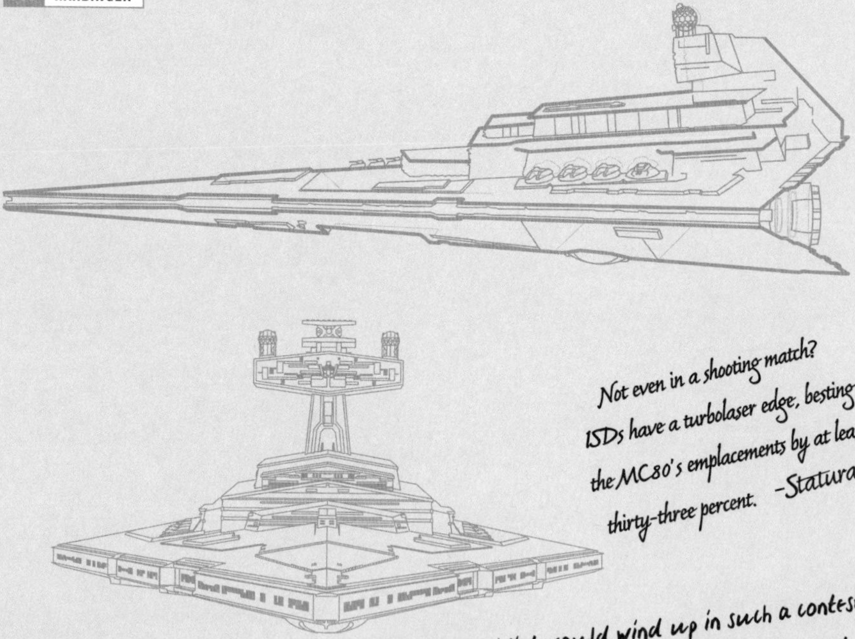

Not even in a shooting match? ISDs have a turbolaser edge, besting the MC80's emplacements by at least thirty-three percent. -Statura

Only an idiot would wind up in such a contest! Mon Cala craft are well rounded. You can't shoot your way through everything! Admiral Ackbar

GEN. DONDONNA TO MON MOTHMA

The Mid Rim Offensive has stalled, and a large part of the blame is the inability of our army commanders to coordinate their efforts on a sector level once they've become mired in ground battles. A mobile starfighter unit like Rogue Squadron will help break this paralysis by relaying reports and attacking targets of opportunity. See attached.

CLASSIFIED DOCUMENT—CLEARANCE LEVEL: 

RIEEKAN/MOTHMA PROG41256

RI 054-X1

MID RIM RETREAT

TO: COMMANDER MOTHMA

FROM: GENERAL RIEEKAN

With regret, I must report that the Mid Rim Offensive has collapsed around several flash points, necessitating the withdrawal of Alliance troops to better-fortified holdings.

The Alliance is abandoning the following worlds, and we expect Imperial forces to regain control in short order:

- Jeyell
- Pothor
- Trasse
- Ord Tiddell
- Charros
- Durkteel

MADE IT OUT ON THE LAST TRANSPORT. AS WE LIFTED OFF, I SAW THE EMPIRE LIGHT UP THE LAUNCHPAD WITH PLASMIC ARTILLERY.
– EMATT

A few local revolutionaries are evacuating with our Alliance troops, but most are remaining on planet to harass the new arrivals. Look for a follow-up report from General Draven regarding the changed political and military outlook in the Mid Rim.

MOTHMA | JOURNAL ENTRY

No war is truly bloodless, but as moral beings we must minimize bloodshed where we can. With our setbacks in the Mid Rim, could espionage be a better path?

We lost most of our deep-cover bureaucrats and sympathetic lawmakers with dissolution of the Imperial Senate.

Now we must start over. At my urging, General Cracken is stepping up the role of Alliance Intelligence. We must be cunning, as well as brave.

CLASSIFIED DOCUMENT—CLEARANCE LEVEL: 

CRACKEN/MOTHMA PROG41294

RI 122-X8

UPDATE: IMPERIAL INTELLIGENCE ASSETS

TO: COMMANDER MOTHMA

FROM: GENERAL AIREN CRACKEN, CHIEF OF REBEL INTELLIGENCE

At this time, we have a number of active operatives within the Empire. Some are new, while others have been supplying reliable intel for years. Our roster draws from the Empire's military, its bureaucracy, and its civil government.

Please review the following names and profiles to get a sense of our range concerning future operations.

- Col. Vin Northal
- Lt. Gov. Javor Tallensia
- Lt. Ander Rendrake
- Minister Alfons Allsing
- Col. Ilo Jev
- Maj. Kerri Lessev
- Maj. Tarn Innis
- Gov. Striate Cruch
- Lt. Sarchen Snyle

This is currently on of our most pressing problems with the First Order. They've isolated none of o agents can get insic —Hold

We should also review our plans for extracting these agents should their cover be compromised. The Dragon Void race is a model worth emulating, even though I wouldn't expect Han Solo to pull off the same trick twice.

DOC #6188831-ALL

TO: MON MOTHMA

FROM: GENERAL RIEEKAN

SUBJ: IMPERIAL DEFECTOR WITH 61st MOBILE INFANTRY (TWILIGHT COMPANY)

Hundreds of our battle groups in the Mid Rim are now in retreat. Amid the bad news, the commanding officer of Twilight Company reports that he has a lead on an intelligence asset that could let us resist the Empire's momentum.

Haidoral Prime's Imperial governor, Everi Chalis, has offered to defect on the condition that we guarantee her immunity from prosecution. In exchange, she's offering detailed information on the Empire's logistics and supply operations in the Mid Rim and beyond.

Given his understanding of supply chains, General Grafis has agreed to vet the governor's intel. If this information proves valid, we may wish to bring the governor in for a meeting with High Command.

This data proved its value, and it helped legitimize the use of Bothan intel on the second Death Star. I'm not sure whether to praise this development or condemn it. —Leia

CLASSIFIED DOCUMENT—CLEARANCE LEVEL:

SEERTAY/ONORAN PROG41299

RI 187-S9

UPDATE: IMPERIAL INTELLIGENCE ASSETS

TO: GENERAL ONORAN, SPECFORCES

FROM: COL. ANNA SEERTAY

Please read the recommendation from one of our scouts concerning an Alliance headquarters location. I agree with most of her points, but you should know that Corporal Purpruff is a Gigoran. So when she says "clean and brisk," keep in mind that the temperatures on this planet are well below freezing even in full daylight.

CONTINUED

I KNEW PURPRUFF! THE SHRIKES AND THE VAPETAILERS USED TO HOLD PAZAAK MATCHES OVER CANTINA CHITS. I LATER SAW HER NAME AMONG THE FALLEN OF ECHO BASE.
- EMATT

SCOUTING LOG ENTRY

FILED BY: Cpl. Purpruff, Vapetailers unit, Alliance SpecForces

RECON FILE

Hoth

STANDARD GRID: K-18

STELLAR REGION: Ison Corridor

SYSTEM: Hoth

ORBITAL BODY: Hoth, sixth orbital shell

CLIMATE: Standard breathable, subzero temp

TERRAIN: Glaciers, mountains, frozen seas, snowfields, cavern networks

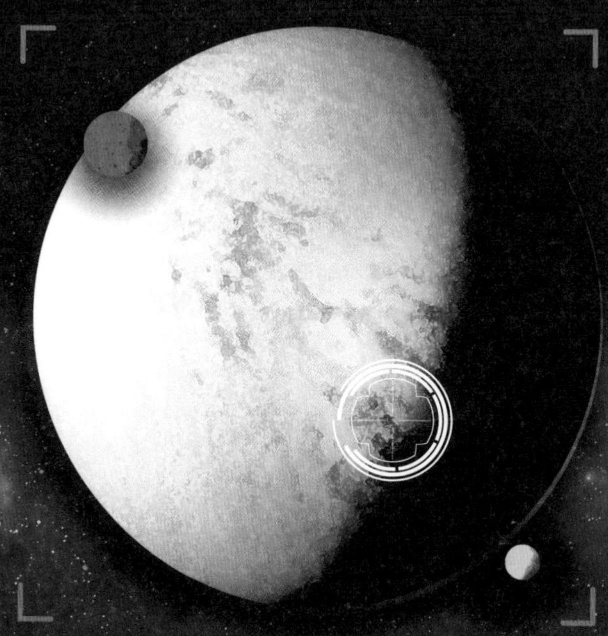

NOTES: Planetary body is not officially charted. Absent from both Nav Guild release 5572.C5 and Giju plot 773/B. Is unofficially known to smugglers (see Cynabar shadowgrids X11–X22) but has been largely ignored. Possesses no material or mineral value, and climate is unpleasant to most organics.

ORBITAL IMPRESSIONS:

- It is an easy hyperjump to Ison Corridor and Corellian Trade Spine.
- Asteroid field is a nav hazard. Random ships that jump in-system probably won't stick around.
- There is a surprisingly high incidence of meteorites reaching surface, though that does provide cover for starship traffic.
- Sensors indicate planet is tectonically stable.

CONTINUED

SURFACE IMPRESSIONS:

- Atmosphere clean and brisk. Air exquisitely tingled my nostrils after so many weeks of cabin recycling.
- What a beautiful expanse! Blue above, white below—the perfect horizon.
- Terrain mapper indicated a huge cavern warren near my landing spot. I hiked to the closest entrance to explore. Inside I found ice palaces big enough to house star freighters.
- Planted a sticky mine on a stalactite to test the cavern's structural integrity. Not even a shudder when it detonated. This ice is rock solid.
- Life-form scanners led me to these cuties. They didn't scatter when I approached, and they ate out of my hand when I offered a ration stick. Might be useful for hauling gear or carrying riders. They smell nice too.
- Note that if maintaining water in its liquid state is important, artificial heating will be required.

END DOCUMENT

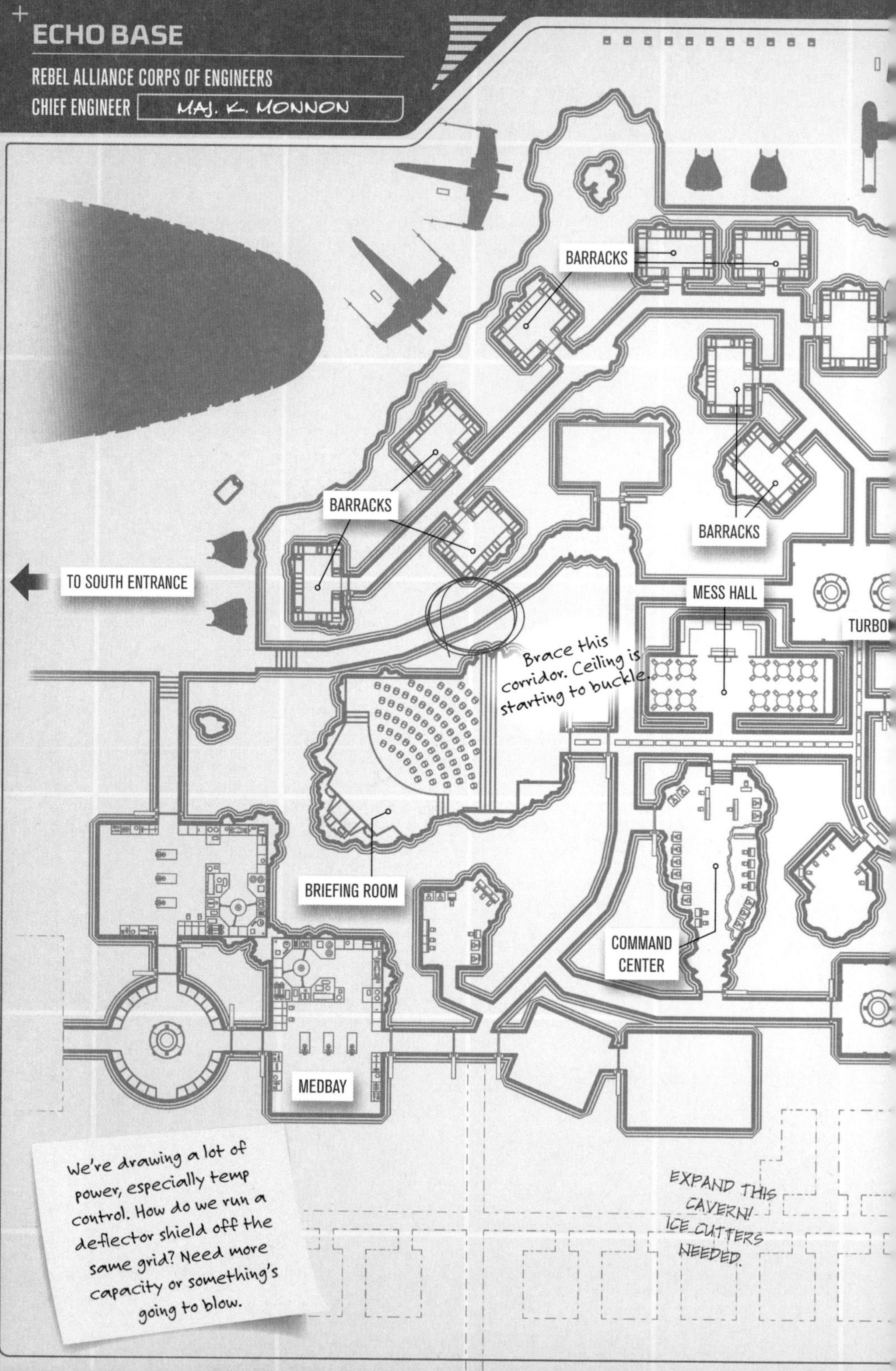
ECHO BASE
REBEL ALLIANCE CORPS OF ENGINEERS
CHIEF ENGINEER
MAJ. K. MONNON
BARRACKS
BARRACKS
BARRACKS
TO SOUTH ENTRANCE
MESS HALL
TURBO
Brace this corridor. Ceiling is starting to buckle.
BRIEFING ROOM
COMMAND CENTER
MEDBAY
We're drawing a lot of power, especially temp control. How do we run a deflector shield off the same grid? Need more capacity or something's going to blow.
EXPAND THIS CAVERN! ICE CUTTERS NEEDED.

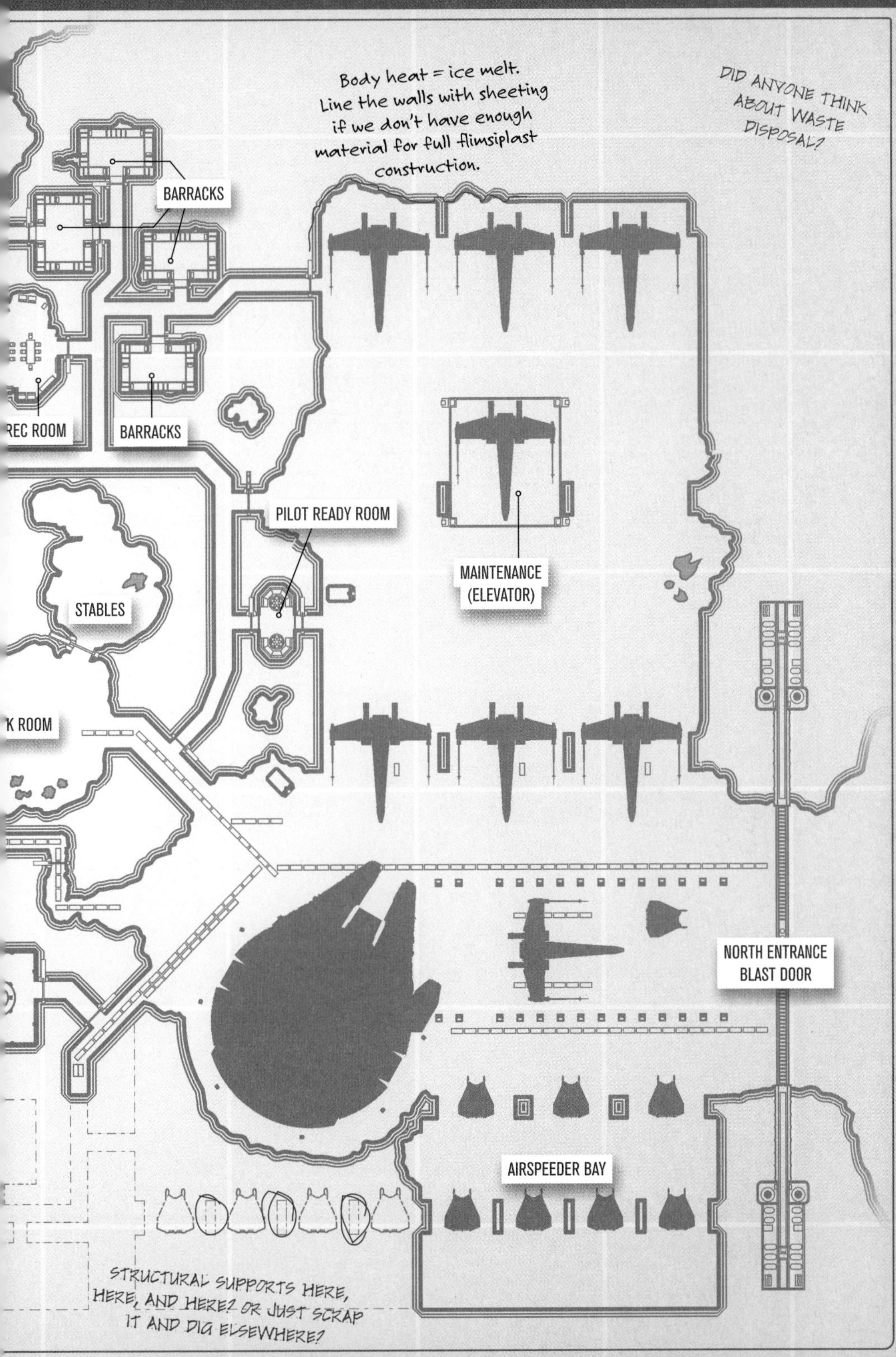
Body heat = ice melt.
Line the walls with sheeting if we don't have enough material for full flimsiplast construction.
DID ANYONE THINK ABOUT WASTE DISPOSAL?
BARRACKS
REC ROOM
BARRACKS
PILOT READY ROOM
STABLES
MAINTENANCE (ELEVATOR)
K ROOM
NORTH ENTRANCE BLAST DOOR
AIRSPEEDER BAY
STRUCTURAL SUPPORTS HERE, HERE, AND HERE? OR JUST SCRAP IT AND DIG ELSEWHERE?

HENDRI UNDERHOLT

Hoth? Whose idea was Hoth? The tip of my nose aches and I think I've lost feeling in my fingers!

MON MOTHMA

It's precisely Hoth's inhospitable climate that makes it so likely to go unnoticed.

HENDRI UNDERHOLT

I'm honored to be your representative, but yesterday I let a bowl of broth sit too long and an ice shell formed.

MON MOTHMA

You know, I considered sending Hostis in your place. But everyone assured me he was already quite chilly.

HENDRI UNDERHOLT

Did you just . . . make a joke? Commander, I'm stunned.

MON MOTHMA

Savor the moment. I'm not making a habit of it.

DOC #6254431-ALL

TO: ALL ECHO BASE PERSONNEL

FROM: GENERAL RIEEKAN

SUBJ: COMM SILENCE AND BASE SECURITY

ALL PERSONNEL MUST READ THIS NOTICE

FAILURE TO COMPLY WILL RESULT IN DISCIPLINARY ACTION

Echo Base is now our home. We would like to avoid a repeat of the Yavin evacuation. All personnel must be diligent in following security protocols to ensure our survival.

- **No communications—outgoing or incoming—for any reason.** Only base-issued gear may be used for sending on-planet messages. ONLY ECHO BASE OTC IS AUTHORIZED TO SEND LONG-RANGE TRANSMISSIONS.
- **No unrestricted hyperspace approaches.** All ship traffic must follow the randomized jump schedule coordinated by High Command. Ships arriving with the wrong approach vector will be flagged as red-level threats.

I warned Rieekan about this. The probe droid must have come from somewhere! Why was there no hyperspace signature? —Admiral Ackbar

Out-system reversion followed by a stealth approach that mimicked an asteroid or meteoroid? —Statura

T-47 AIRSPEEDER:
ECHO BASE SNOWSPEEDER CUSTOMIZATION

MANUFACTURER: Incom Corporation
LENGTH: 5.3 meters
ATMOSPHERIC SPEED: 650 km/hr
FLIGHT CEILING: 175 meters

- Laser cannon
- Forward fuel tanks
- Cabin air inlet
- Power couplings
- Heat dispersion fins
- Harpoon and tow cable

No, no, not the T-47! I can fly anything, but that doesn't mean I want to. Piloting the T-47 is like steering a block of wood.
-Poe

BUG LOG: COLD-WEATHER MODIFICATIONS

T-47 ENGINE COMPONENTS REQUIRE COOLING-FLUID CYCLING TO PREVENT OVERHEATING. BUT OPEN-AIR TEMPS ON HOTH FREEZE THE FLUID AND PREVENT CYCLING.

ENTRY 1

Okay, but does the engine still overheat when exposed to open-air temps? Even without the coolant cycling, the subzero surroundings should offset overheating.

ENTRY 2

Yes, the engine still overheats, or I wouldn't be putting it in the bug log. The repulsorcoil casing is a sealed unit. It gets hot in there.

ENTRY 3

So forget about the liquid coolant and instead try cracking open the repulsorcoil casing.

ENTRY 4

So you want to freeze the engine? You're just replacing one problem with its exact opposite.

ENTRY 5

No, first insulate the repulsorcoil with plastine spray. Then bore a hole in the casing and insert a baffle for increased airflow at high speeds when the engine is overtaxed.

ENTRY 6

Worth a shot. Need a pilot to test it though.

ENTRY 7

Hobbie will do it. Hobbie always does it. Use a tauntaun sledge to haul the speeder back if he crashes.

GENERAL RIEEKAN TO COMMANDER MOTHMA

Our scouting reports didn't indicate the presence of any predators on Hoth, but something is attacking our animal stable. Will keep you apprised of any new developments.

BIOLOGICAL ANALYSIS
UNIT: 2-1B, SURGICAL AND MEDICAL DROID
AFFILIATION: REBEL ALLIANCE, ECHO BASE
MODE: FORENSICS

SUBJECT: Dead tauntaun.

OBJECTIVE: Determine method of death and develop recommendations for preventing Echo Base's organics from suffering same.

ANALYSIS: Blood spatter considerable.

- Identified three distinct gashes between 20–26 cm. in length. Depth of wounds indicates implement(s) had a minimum length of 10 cm.
- Angles of wounds indicate attacker was significantly taller than a tauntaun, possibly bipedal.
- Internal tauntaun organs missing. Presumably eaten.

CONCLUSION: If this predator can inflict this level of trauma on a tauntaun, it can easily do the same to a human or other soft organic.

Chewie and I had to deal with this problem head-on. We found a way to lock up wampas without killing them, but I doubt it would have worked if Echo Base had faced an all-hands predator raid.
—Leia

CLASSIFIED DOCUMENT—CLEARANCE LEVEL:

HARINAR/RIEEKAN PROG41499

RI 119-X1

PROBE DROID ANALYSIS

TO: GENERAL RIEEKAN

FROM: MAJOR HARINAR

AND BY THE TIME WE BLAST THEM, IT'S TOO LATE. PROBOTS HAVE GOT ZERO SENSE OF SELF-PRESERVATION BEYOND GETTING THEIR TATTLETALE TRANSMISSIONS INTO SUBSPACE.
-POE

We recovered the wreckage of the probe droid from perimeter zone 12.

ECHO BASE PERIMETER PATROL REPORT

Incident No.: C241-6501-7731

Type of Incident: Suspected surveillance

Location of recovery: Zone 12

Recovered by: Captain Han Solo, Chewbacca (first mate)

Description of evidence: When discovered, device self-destructed. This action destroyed several critical components including data recorder, central processor, and transmitter. Surviving fragments indicate it was a Viper probe droid: manufacturer Arakyd, model number likely between X0037 and X0172.

This is the tactic the First Order chooses to emphasize? Probe droids have become a weekly nuisance for Resistance fleet elements.
-Holdo

Analysis of the pieces and the recorded transmissions that came from the unit are enough to confirm the droid's Imperial affiliation.

I know what this entails, so I don't say it lightly: Echo Base is compromised.

DOC #6522720-ALL

TO: LEIA ORGANA

FROM: GENERAL RIEEKAN

SUBJ: WHAT HAPPENS NEXT

Princess, we have little choice but to run. The Empire will be here soon enough.

An orbital bombardment is unlikely. Our energy shield will hold up under sustained assault. That means a ground attack. If they follow standard Imperial procedure, they'll land armored cavalry or heavy tanks outside the shield perimeter, and proceed on land until their long-range cannons can target the shield generator.

Once that's down, orbital bombardment and/or troop landings will begin.

When I wrote this, the Imperial fleet hadn't arrived. A lot of us hoped it wouldn't show up at all, that we were raising our heart rates over nothing. That's when the Imperial Death Squadron jumped into Sector 4. —Leia

DOC #6824127-ALL

TO: ALL ECHO BASE DUTY CHIEFS

FROM: LEIA ORGANA

SUBJ: K-1-0 EVAC: DELAYING ACTION AND LAUNCH PROCEDURES

OFFICIAL DOCUMENT

PLAN K-1-0 IS NOW IN EFFECT.

Pilots:

Groups 7 and 10 will operate the T-47s against Imperial ground attack. All other pilots will assemble at the south slope transport launch.

Soldiers:

Echo Base troopers and Alliance army personnel will take up positions within the north ridge trench network and operate the defensive turrets. Echo Station 5-7 will

CONTINUED

coordinate battlefield operations. Alliance marines and SpecForces personnel are to escort the transport crews.

Shield:
The base's energy shield will be activated at the first sign of hyperspace disturbance and will remain at full strength from that point on, with the exception of transport launches as noted below.

Transport schedule:
Once a transport captain has indicated a vessel is fully loaded, Echo Base evacuation control will give the clearance for launch. Two starfighters will accompany each transport.

- To allow passage, the energy shield will be lowered for a few seconds only. Maintain a tight formation and closely monitor your instruments.
- Echo Base ion control will fire several blasts along the flight path to discourage Imperial vessels from taking up intercept vectors. Starfighter escorts are to provide additional protection as needed.
- Once the transport and its escorts are clear of the Imperial cordon, they will jump to hyperspace and follow coded instructions toward the fleet rendezvous.

Final pullout:
When a majority of transports have launched, Echo Base control will issue the evacuation code signal. All remaining personnel are to make an orderly withdrawal to the south slope and depart Hoth aboard the final starfighters and transports.

We've trained for this. We're ready. We'll be together again very soon.

May the Force be with us.

END DOCUMENT

I got the call of course, but there wasn't enough time to scramble the fleet and get to Hoth. The actual evacuation occurred in a matter of hours.

Admiral Ackbar

CLASSIFIED DOCUMENT—CLEARANCE LEVEL:

ANTILLES/NA'AL PROG41620

RI 087-R2

ACTION ON HOTH

TO: ARCHIVIST NA'AL

FROM: LT. ANTILLES (RED 3)

I'M FEELING THIS. BUT TO ACCEPT ALL THESE FAC AND STILL FLY AGAINST HEAVY AT-ATS? THE ROGUES WERE AS CRAZY AS EVERYBODY SAYS. -POE

Honestly, we weren't ready. Our T-47 snowspeeders weren't equipped to go up against armor. They were really just punched-up cargo haulers. These were Blizzard Force AT-ATs, shielded against weather and wind, able to shrug off hundreds of hits.

At first, I thought we might do some damage by focusing on weak points at the neck and knees. But small targets are hard to hit when you're juking through flak.

Tripping the walkers was something we'd always discussed, but actually doing it was an admission that our primary tactics had failed. Let me explain what goes into a successful trip: an unaided precision shot from a rear-facing harpoon immediately followed by a tight and predictable turn that exposes the ship to enemy cannons.

Janson, my gunner, secured a firm hold on the walker's leg with his first shot. Amazing. But for the next half minute, I had to keep our speeder tipped up on its side and our speed steady as we looped the cable. Too wide and we'd snap it; too close and we'd clip a leg. Release it too soon and the walker would break the tangle; fly too long and eventually somebody'd put a blast through our canopy.

EXACTLY! MADMEN! -POE

If the AT-AT's commander hadn't pushed ahead, he might have stayed upright. But when the body lurched past the tipping point, the whole machine flopped chin first into the snow.

Once down, the neck joint target was exposed! A couple shots to the neck coil punctured the reactor. The AT-AT went up before a single snowtrooper could crawl from its hatch.

Is the same trick going to work next time? Maybe not. If the Empire's smart, they'll institute new engagement protocols. But I'll count our wins wherever we can.

CONTINUED

SUB AT-AT TRIPPING MANEUVER

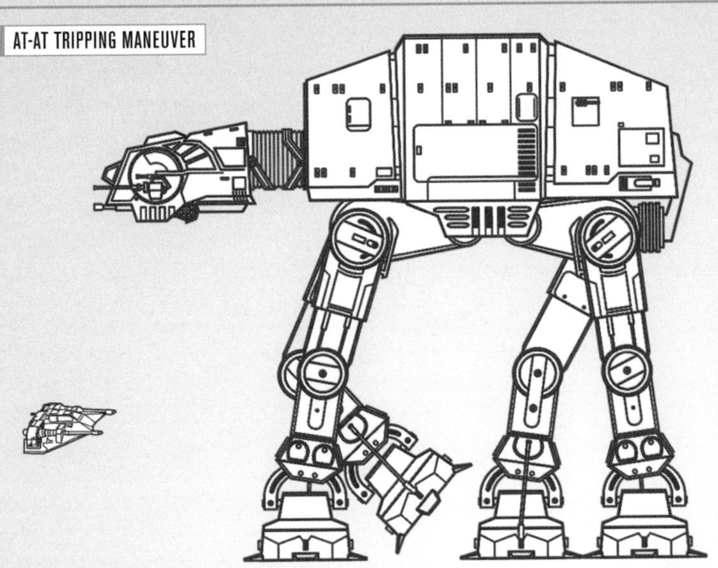

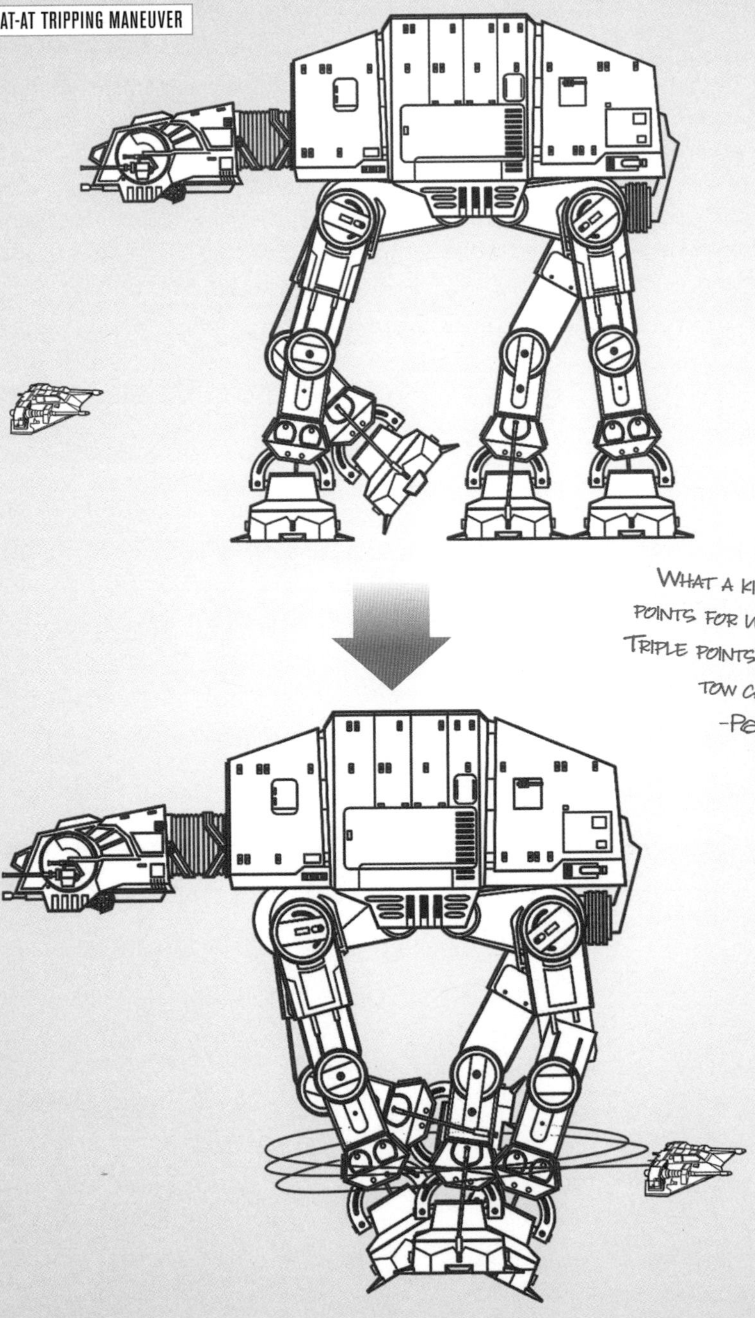

WHAT A KILL! DOUBLE POINTS FOR USING A T-47. TRIPLE POINTS FOR USING A TOW CABLE!
-POE

CARLIST RIEEKAN TO MON MOTHMA

We'd been there less than a month. We'd launched a hundred small projects to make Hoth's hostile environment something livable and familiar. And suddenly none of it mattered.

Why was the probot there at all? Did we miss a tracker or fail to shake a tail? Did the Force have other plans for us that day?

I don't know the answers. I do know that we saved lives during the pullout. The dead will receive appropriate honors.

IN MEMORIAM

The Fallen of Echo Base

With great sorrow we commemorate the deaths of our friends and comrades killed in the line of duty at Echo Base during the evacuation of Hoth.

All of those who perished had only recently been assigned to the new headquarters, and all did their duty in the face of overwhelming opposition. We owe our lives to their sacrifice.

A multifaith ceremony of remembrance will be held tomorrow in Hangar A aboard the Home One *at 1100 hours.*

LOTS OF NAMES WEREN'T INCLUDED IN THIS SERVICE BECAUSE NO ONE COULD DETERMINE IF THEY'D DIED ON HOTH OR MISREPORTED IN THE LOGS. – EMATT

TO: The free peoples of the galaxy
FROM: Mon Mothma of the Rebel Alliance

The Rebellion did not win the day at Hoth, that much is true. I value the facts too much to deceive you. Contrast this with the Empire's claims of an unprecedented, galaxy-changing victory, and ask yourself—who is telling the truth?

Does honesty win converts? Now that I'm starting a new Resistance from scratch, I certainly hope so. —Leia

FACT:

The Rebel Alliance evacuated our headquarters on Hoth at the first sign of Imperial attackers. Though we suffered losses, every member of High Command escaped unharmed.

FACT:

The Alliance fleet, not present at Hoth, is as strong as ever. We have since won victories against the Empire at Pyros and Mirrin Prime.

FACT:

Our ranks continue to grow as more and more freethinkers realize the hollowness of Imperial ideology.

Remember, a life spent in service to a dictator benefits only the dictator. Join us in the Alliance to Restore the Republic, where every being has a voice.

COMPNOR

FOR IMMEDIATE RELEASE

THE EMPIRE MARCHES ON: OUTER RIM TRIUMPH PUTS THE REBELS ON THE RUN

Hoth—A desolate ice ball in the wilds of the southern Rim is the site of the latest Imperial victory, where military forces under the command of Lord Darth Vader annihilated a rebel nest and exterminated many key leaders of the insurgency.

"After fleeing in the face of the Empire's Mid Rim advance, the rebels sought refuge on a hostile frozen world," exulted Yupe Tashu, special advisor to the Emperor. "Yet even there they could not escape justice."

A combined military effort pinned the rebels in place following the Empire's surprise emergence from hyperspace. As their enemy scrambled in panic, the hardened professionals of the Imperial Army's Blizzard Force mowed down the meager defenders.

Some of the Empire's most-wanted criminals, including Princess Leia Organa of Alderaan, are believed to have been present at the engagement. Their deaths have not yet been confirmed, but Imperial commanders are justifiably celebrating this stunning blow against those who seek to undermine galactic security.

Mon Mothma,

ALLIANCE MINISTER OF FINANCE

Let me state upfront: I am, of course, grateful for the sacrifice of those who perished on Hoth.

With that out of the way, may I please call your attention to the KDY v-150 Planet Defender ion cannon we left behind. This weapon had a significant credit value attached to it, specifically 978,900 (accounting for depreciation).

How many times did we fire it? A dozen? The Alliance is now authorizing 81,000-credit expenditures per shot?

I am not arguing the decision to leave it behind; I am questioning the fiscal sanity of those who thought we should install it there in the first place. It wasn't modular; it wasn't mobile. Our engineers spent a month hollowing out an ice chamber to accommodate its capacitor banks. That's an additional expense I haven't even accounted for yet.

CONTINUED

Not to throw cold water on the recent good news, but the capture of four fully loaded transports in the Pyros system is hardly sufficient to balance the accounts, given the irreplaceability of our lost asset.

This recklessness must stop! Our reserves are exhausted. Our liquidity is entirely dependent on loans. I shouldn't have to tell you that the goodwill of creditors is a fickle thing.

Sincerely,

Senator Nower Jebel

Senator Nower Jebel
ALLIANCE MINISTER OF FINANCE

Was it recovered? The ion cannon? —Holdo

Sometime after Endor, I believe it was. But the elements had ravaged its internals. —Leia

DOC #6855326-ALL

TO: ALL ALLIANCE FLEET COMMANDERS

FROM: ADMIRAL ACKBAR

SUBJ: MOBILE RENDEZVOUS COORDINATES AND JUMP PROTOCOL

To reduce fuel burn while maximizing operational security, the Alliance fleet will henceforth shift to a jump schedule once every two cycles.

Jump coordinates for the rendezvous will be transmitted from *Home One* to nearby ships of the fleet. From there, the coordinates will be relayed to outposts, vessels, and intelligence agents across the galaxy using regional and temporal encryption protocols.

Any ship that arrives at the rendezvous spot but does not emerge from hyperspace on the correct reversion vector will be targeted by every gunner in the fleet.

Please ensure you have followed the rendezvous protocols down to the last detail. If not, we cannot be held responsible for your vaporization.

Admiral Ackbar

And I don't regret this one bit. We could use this attitude today, showing these new pilots we mean business.

WITH TURBOLASERS? HONESTLY, I THINK WE'D GET THE MESSAGE WITH JUST A VERBAL WARNING. —POE

This unfinished art is a sobering reminder of Hendri's and this collection's fate.

—Leia

SHELL TOP-LEVEL/CATEGORY

ALLIANCE CHRON 4

ABSTRACT:

Counterattack

Hendri Underholt

ARCHIVIST

STANDARD DATE: 22 AFE

(AFTER THE FORMATION OF THE EMPIRE)

SHELL ACTIVE AND ONGOING

MOTHMA | JOURNAL ENTRY

On my orders, the Alliance has remained on the move since the evacuation of Echo Base. We can't afford to lose more heavy emplacements or risk the capture of command staff, and we certainly can't hand the Empire another propaganda victory like Hoth.

We are safer on the move. But when we're invisible to the Empire, our allies don't see us either. If the galaxy doesn't see bold action from the Alliance, its citizens will pin their hopes elsewhere.

Our name is the Alliance to Restore the Republic. We will never attain that goal by retreating from the centers of power.

It's amazing how much a single planet can provide legitimacy even if you held a thousand worlds prior to that conquest.
—Leia

QUEEN OF THE CORE NETWORK

NEWS OF THE NEW ORDER

Is the Alliance Finished?

By Tracene Kane

Imperial City, Coruscant—The Rebel Alliance doesn't have long to live. That's the tantalizing picture painted by senior Imperial advisor Mas Amedda, in exclusive statements made to Queen of the Core Network. Amedda's remarks occurred during the second day of the annual media summit at the Imperial Palace.

"Their leadership is in shambles," confided Amedda, as servers cleared plates of chilled Bellassan peppers. "Half of them can't wait to sell out the other half for the reward money. And their fleet is recklessly burning fuel."

Leaning closer, Amedda added "All we have to do is blow and the rebellion will come tumbling down."

Empty gossip masquerading as genuine information. No matter which government holds the galaxy, this problem never goes away.
—Holdo

CLASSIFIED DOCUMENT—CLEARANCE LEVEL: 

ACKBAR/MOTHMA PROG41789

RI 021-CT7

COUNTERATTACK PROPOSAL: KUAT DRIVE YARDS (OPERATION RINGBREAKER)

TO: COMMANDER MOTHMA

FROM: ADMIRAL ACKBAR

Commander, a dramatic counterattack is imperative to reverse our flow. Galactic dominance is built upon naval power. Though the Empire outnumbers us, it is within our power to poison their spawning beds.

"Operation Ringbreaker" has been vetted by Alliance Intelligence. Its goal is to shut down of the naval shipyards at Kuat—a prime military stronghold in the Imperial Core. Operation Ringbreaker would be a succession of coordinated assaults, each designed to drain Kuat's defenses as it dispatches warships in response.

Once the defenses in the Kuat sector have been stretched to the snapping point, we will attack with naval and infantry forces, severing comm links and inflicting catastrophic damage to manufacturing hubs.

I cannot speak to the specifics of the industrial sabotage, for that is Madine's lane to swim. But as your naval commander, I can assure you that nothing would hurt the Empire more than dozens of stricken megaplants venting superheated gas into space.

It was a brilliantly planned attack, brought low by undetectable hazards! Had we made it to Kuat, we could have shaved a year off the war.
Admiral Ackbar

Surely it would have taken many months to feel the repercussions of the production slowdown?
-Statura

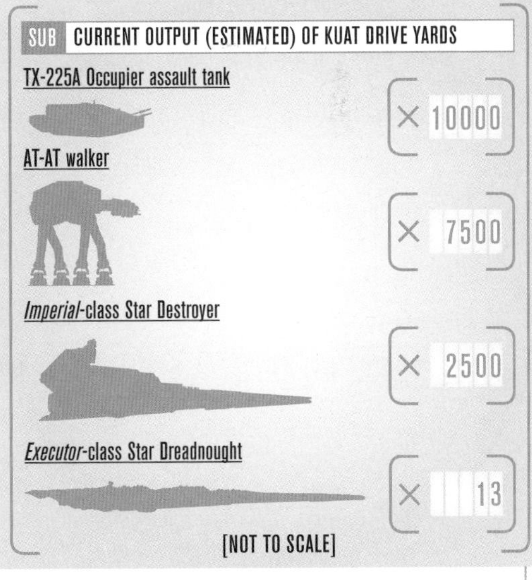

CLASSIFIED DOCUMENT—CLEARANCE LEVEL: 

MADINE/ACKBAR PROG41821

RI 045-CT7

OPERATION RINGBREAKER PHASE 1

TO: ADMIRAL ACKBAR

FROM: GENERAL MADINE

PHASE 1 OVERVIEW

Deplete Kuat's defenses through targeted attacks on Imperial holdings.

Each of the following sites produces rare ores, armor-grade polymers, or other war resources. Hitting these targets will also advance our secondary objective of supply-chain disruption.

Alliance forces led by the 61st Mobile Infantry will secure the following targets in succession:

- Mardona III
- The moon of Obumubo
- The dockyards of Najan-Rovi
- Nakadia
- Naator
- Xagobah
- The Kuliquo belt
- Inyusu Tor on Sullust
- Malastare

Most of these are in the possession of the New Republic, but since the disarmament few are actually producing anything we can use. —Holdo

PHASE 2 AND BEYOND

Operation Ringbreaker will culminate with the sabotage of Kuat Drive Yards. See attached documentation concerning Kuat operations and statistics on shipyard capacity and output.

A complete Alliance battle plan for the Kuat attack is forthcoming.

DOC #7122423-ALL

TO: CMDR MOTHMA

FROM: GENERAL MADINE

SUBJ: SHIPYARD DISRUPTION

With Operation Ringbreaker meeting with early success, I feel our current angle of attack could provide a broader path to victory. This map notes the locations of other major Imperial shipyards and drydocks, as well as key mining centers for metals and ores. Once we take out Kuat, these should be our next targets.

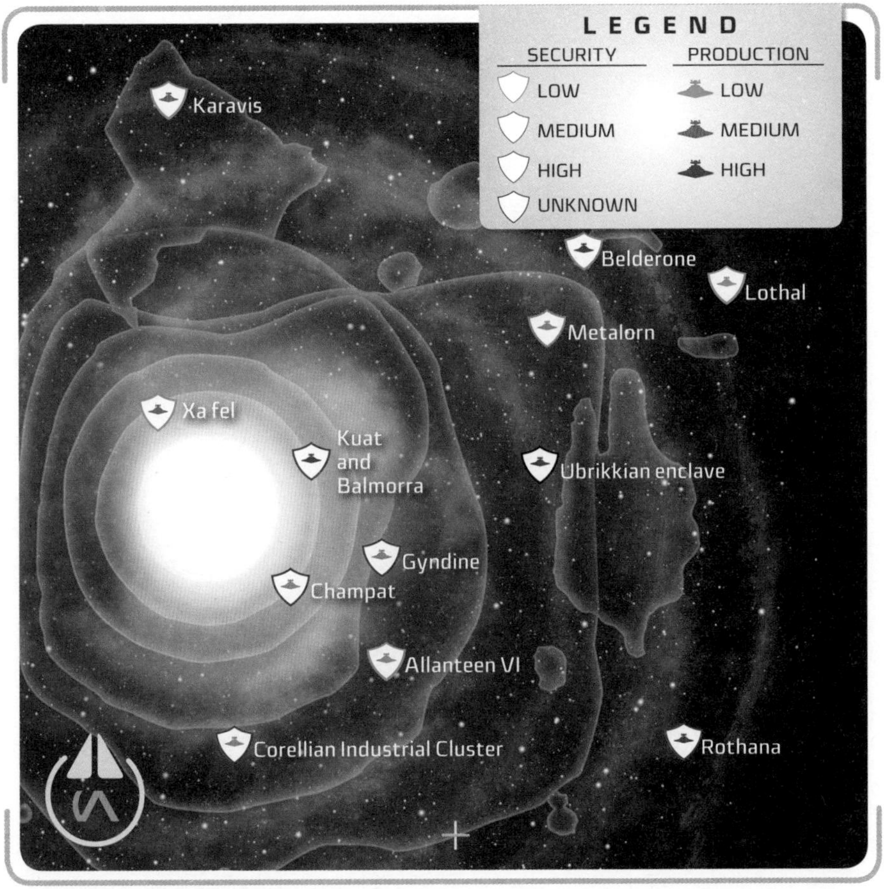

LEGEND

SECURITY	PRODUCTION
LOW	LOW
MEDIUM	MEDIUM
HIGH	HIGH
UNKNOWN	

Karavis
Belderone
Lothal
Metalorn
Xa fel
Kuat and Balmorra
Ubrikkian enclave
Gyndine
Champat
Allanteen VI
Corellian Industrial Cluster
Rothana

DOC #7137552-ALL

TO: CMDR MOTHMA

FROM: GENERAL MADINE

SUBJ: SULLUST ENGAGEMENT (OPERATION RINGBREAKER)

> I WENT TO SULLUST DURING THE LATE STAGES OF THIS SIEGE TO ASSIST THE NATIVE RESISTANCE. AS I RECALL, TWILIGHT COMPANY ALREADY HAD THE SITUATION WELL IN HAND. - EMATT

I regret to inform you that Operation Ringbreaker has stalled at Sullust. Our forces groundside have reported a fierce Imperial counterattack. They are currently bogged down in a protracted siege of the Inyusu Tor refinery complex.

We will support them and evacuate if necessary. But the standoff at Sullust has broken our momentum. Kuat will receive resupply before we can stage our next assault. Our window of opportunity has closed. The final phase of Operation Ringbreaker is a no-go.

ID: 522Z-01
[SOLLUST]

THE FIGHT AT KUAT NEVER HAPPENED, BUT CANCELLING OPERATION RINGBREAKER STILL FELT LIKE A DEFEAT. IF WE HAD ONLY KNOWN MORE ABOUT IMPERIAL STRENGTH NEAR SULLUST WE MIGHT HAVE BEEN READY FOR IT. PERHAPS THAT COULD HAVE PREVENTED OUR CAMPAIGN FROM STUMBLING OVER ITS OWN FEET.

I HAVE ALWAYS BELIEVED THAT THE ALLIANCE IS BETTER SERVED WHEN IT LEANS TOWARD DIPLOMACY AND SUBTERFUGE RATHER THAN MILITARY HEROICS. THE HAIDORAL PRIME DEFECTION AND THE GALEN ERSO LEAK—THESE ARE JUST TWO EXAMPLES OF HOW WE CAN PUT OURSELVES ON EQUAL FOOTING WHEN FACING A BEHEMOTH OF AN ENEMY.

HERE, AT LEAST, I'M WILLING TO ADMIT IT—I DON'T PARTICULARLY LIKE WORKING WITH INTELLIGENCE. THE LIFELONG AGENTS LIKE DRAVEN HAVE A CHILLY MORAL PRAGMATISM THAT THEY CAN USE TO JUSTIFY ANY CRIME.

The biggest danger in a democracy isn't always your enemies. It can come from within, when you choose to make moral calculations on a sliding scale.
—Leia

FORTUNATELY, AIREN CRACKEN IS THE EXCEPTION. I'VE KNOWN AIREN SINCE THE EARLY DAYS. I RESPECT THAT HE'S COMFORTABLE WITH CONTEMPLATING HIS LIMITS. HE ISN'T AFRAID TO TELL ME WHEN OUR INTEL IS INADEQUATE, AND I FEEL THAT NOW IS ONE OF THOSE TIMES.

I WILL NOT LAUNCH ANOTHER KUAT CAMPAIGN ON INCOMPLETE DATA. WE NEED TO PUT MORE EYES ON THE EMPIRE. WE'VE RELIED ON CONTACTS IN HUTT SPACE FOR YEARS, YET WE'VE BARELY TAPPED THE GALAXY'S OTHER INFO-BROKERS—THE OBROANS OR THE BOTHANS, FOR EXAMPLE.

THAT CHANGES TODAY. WE MUST WIDEN THE CONE OF OUR LISTENING AND SHARPEN THE TOOLS OF OUR INVESTIGATION. EVEN IF WE HAVE TO OPEN OUR POCKETBOOK AND HIRE SPIES TO DO IT.

DOC #7238854-ALL

TO: CMDR MOTHMA

FROM: GENERAL MADINE

SUBJ: BOTHANS

You'll be happy to hear that the Bothans have agreed to the intelligence op we've discussed.

I don't disagree with the decision to enlist outside intelligence assets, especially given Tagge's gutting of the underworld and the shambles left in the wake of our Mid Rim pullout. But we must be cautious. We can't verify information that we don't control.

AT THE TIME, MY UNIT WAS TRYING TO DRAW INFORMATION OUT OF DEVARONIAN EXPLORERS. WE WERE PULLED OFF THE ASSIGNMENT WHEN THE BOTHAN DEAL WENT DOWN.
- EMATT

MON MOTHMA TO GEN. MADINE

I understand your concerns, but another Scarif isn't going to fall into our laps. The intelligence coup that led to the Battle of Yavin is the only thing that kept us in the game. Without it, the Alliance would have remained ignorant until the end.

GEN. MADINE TO MON MOTHMA

I know. I was there. But the Alliance can be equally harmed by jumping at false positives.

MON MOTHMA TO GEN. MADINE

We need to take action if we are to end this war. Work with the Bothans, General. Your first job is to verify the rumors coming out of the Moddell sector. I'll authorize the expense.

<<ALLIANCE DECRYPT V88//WEEMS//SUBSPACE TRANSCEIVER INTERCEPT>>

INTERCEPTED TRANSMISSION

ATTENTION ALL FLEET AND GARRISON COMMANDERS

FLAG LIEUTENANT EDWIG ON BEHALF OF ADMIRAL PIETT, FLEET COMMAND

BE ALERT

Enemy espionage is probable within your sector or oversector. Imperial Intelligence has issued a credible warning of covert rebel action. In response, all information security categories are to be increased by one full level.

CURRENTLY AT RISK:

- Fleet movements
- Cargo schedules
- Cargo manifests
- Sector communications
- Officer postings
- Command passkeys
- Codebreaker strings

BE WARY OF:

- Guild-affiliated or independent databrokers
- Local infochats on the urban or planetary level
- Agents of the Bothan Spynet
- Members of the Columi species
- Herglic traders
- Any and all cranial cyborgs
- Known rebel agents
- Suspected rebel agents
- Potential rebel agents

Your ISB liason has more detailed information and will provide further instructions.

END TRANSMISSION

One unfortunate side effect: the deaths of the Bothans prevented us from investigating the origin and viability of the data they brought us. —Leia

DOC #7325162-AL

TO: CMDR MOTHMA

FROM: GENERAL CRACKEN

SUBJ: BOTHAN INTEL OP: FOLLOW-UP

Bothan mission sustained massive loss of life. Madine's team is assembling the chain of events to see what went wrong. Despite it all, we got the information we wanted. But at a very high cost.

Delto and Weems have teams analyzing the data now. It looks like the Moddell sector was the correct hunch. Construction of an Imperial megastructure is taking place in the sector at a remote moon called Endor (a shipwreck magnet and a castaway exile for old spacers). Definitely a battle station, though I'll let the techs confirm whether it is what I think it is.

There's something else worth stressing: Endor appears to be a command hub. The SSD *Executor* is a frequent visitor, which means Vader and Fleet Admiral Piett are probably there too. And it looks like Emperor Palpatine might be vacationing at Endor, overseeing the final phase of the battle station's construction in person.

Below is what we know about the officer in charge of the battle station—which is not much yet.

1

NAME:

Jerjerrod, Tiaan

RANK: Rear Admiral, Moff
BIRTHWORLD: Tinnel IV
HEIGHT: 1.7 meters
WEIGHT: 75 kg
STANDARD AGE: 39 standard years
MEMBERSHIPS: COMPNOR, Emperor's Boosters, Keep the Core Secure, Taung & Zhell Society (University of Coruscant)

MADINE/MOTHMA PROG42000

RI 033-X4

DEATH STAR MK. 2

TO: COMMANDER MOTHMA

FROM: GENERAL MADINE

Here's what we've decrypted from the Bothan score so far. It's another Death Star, no doubt about it. Taking shape at Endor, southern Rim, Moddell sector. See enclosed report from Col. Delto in Intelligence.

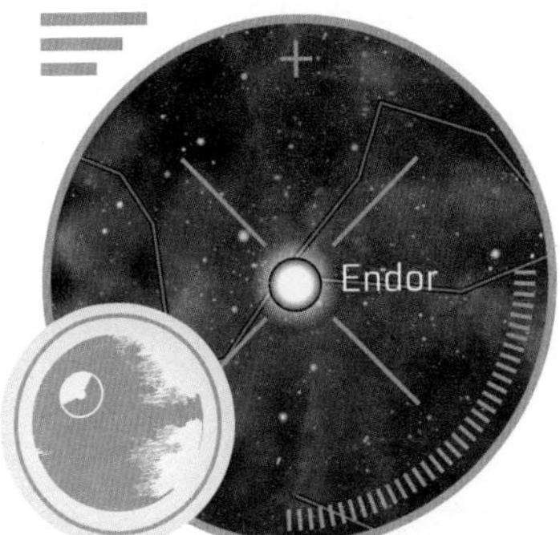

We don't know when they started, but if the telemetry is accurate they definitely haven't finished it yet. That means we have to attack now. I've seen the list of planets listed as candidates for "suppression of sedition." If we let the Empire finish this superweapon, it's the same as surrendering.

COL. DELTO TO GEN. MADINE

General—Look at the data scans. It's a bigger and better Death Star. We always knew the Empire might build another one, and that they'd fix Galen Erso's exploit when they did.

But this second Death Star is not finished! Look at it, all ragged and lopsided. A half-built Death Star is practically naked!

To explain: hypermatter reactors by their very nature are perma-vulnerable. If there's not an airtight quadanium shell encasing the reactor (that's basically what the superstructure is), our starfighters can fly within torpedo range and light up the works.

We don't need another Erso flaw—not when the guts are lying right there on the table! We don't have to make another miracle shot. This time, we can walk right up to the reactor and punch it.

CONTINUED

CONTINUED

I've read up on this, and it wasn't that easy! The reactor wasn't exposed, even if the superstructure wasn't finished. They're talking about running for kilometers down narrow piping shafts.
-Poe

MADINE/MOTHMA PROG42000

SUB DEATH STAR II

POLE-TO-POLE MAGNETIC SHIELDING

QUADANIUM STEEL HULL

HYPERMATTER REACTOR

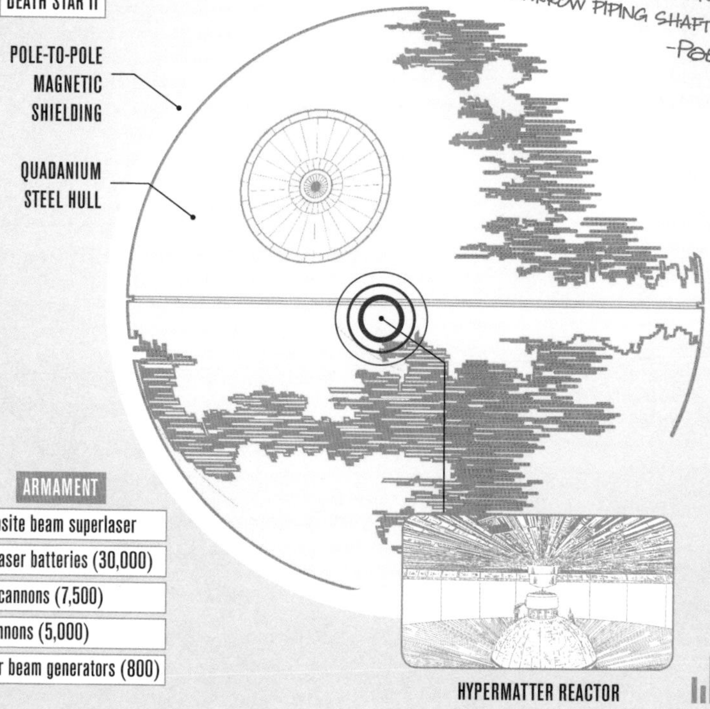

ARMAMENT

Composite beam superlaser
Turbolaser batteries (30,000)
Laser cannons (7,500)
Ion cannons (5,000)
Tractor beam generators (800)

END

END DOCUMENT

CLASSIFIED DOCUMENT—CLEARANCE LEVEL: 

ORGANA/MOTHMA PROG42009

RI 021-D08

OPERATION YELLOW MOON

TO: MON MOTHMA

FROM: LEIA ORGANA

As we discussed in the command staff meeting on Zastiga, I will lead the diversionary expedition in the Corva sector for what we've agreed to call "Operation Yellow Moon."

CONTINUED

ORGANA/MOTHMA PROG42009

Overview:

- Rebel team to place message beacons at locations (Bastille, Sessid, Juresh) in the Corva sector
- Beacons will transmit a coded message urging Alliance forces to rendezvous at Yellow Moon in the Galaan system
- Message will employ an out-of-date Alliance code known to have been broken by Imperial Intelligence

I understand the reasoning behind this operation. We need to draw attention away from our preparations in the Moddell sector, and to do that the Empire must believe that our designs on the Corva sector are legitimate.

But our forces in Corva aren't in on the ruse. They're going to rendezvous at Yellow Moon and the Empire will be waiting for them. We're asking our allies to leap into an ambush.

END DOCUMENT

I questioned this at the time, but now, from a distance of some years, I understand the burden of command. I have been willing to issue an order that I wouldn't execute.
—Leia

MON MOTHMA TO LEIA ORGANA

I'm sorry it has to be this way. I didn't want to go into it on Zastiga, but Mon Cala and Chandrila are the top candidates on the intercepted list of targets for planetary annihilation. We've already lost one world. Some of our fellow a rebels may die, but I am trying to save billions.

DOC #7315582-ALL

TO: CMDR MOTHMA

FROM: ADMIRAL ACKBAR

SUBJ: HYPERSPACE NAVIGATION IN MODDELL SECTOR

You know our fleet can't jump wherever it wishes. We must respect the limitations of hyperspatial physics.

The report below, from one of our Rim scouts, puts the problem into focus. Without a clear approach to Endor, we will forfeit the element of surprise.

CONTINUED

DOC #7315582-ALL

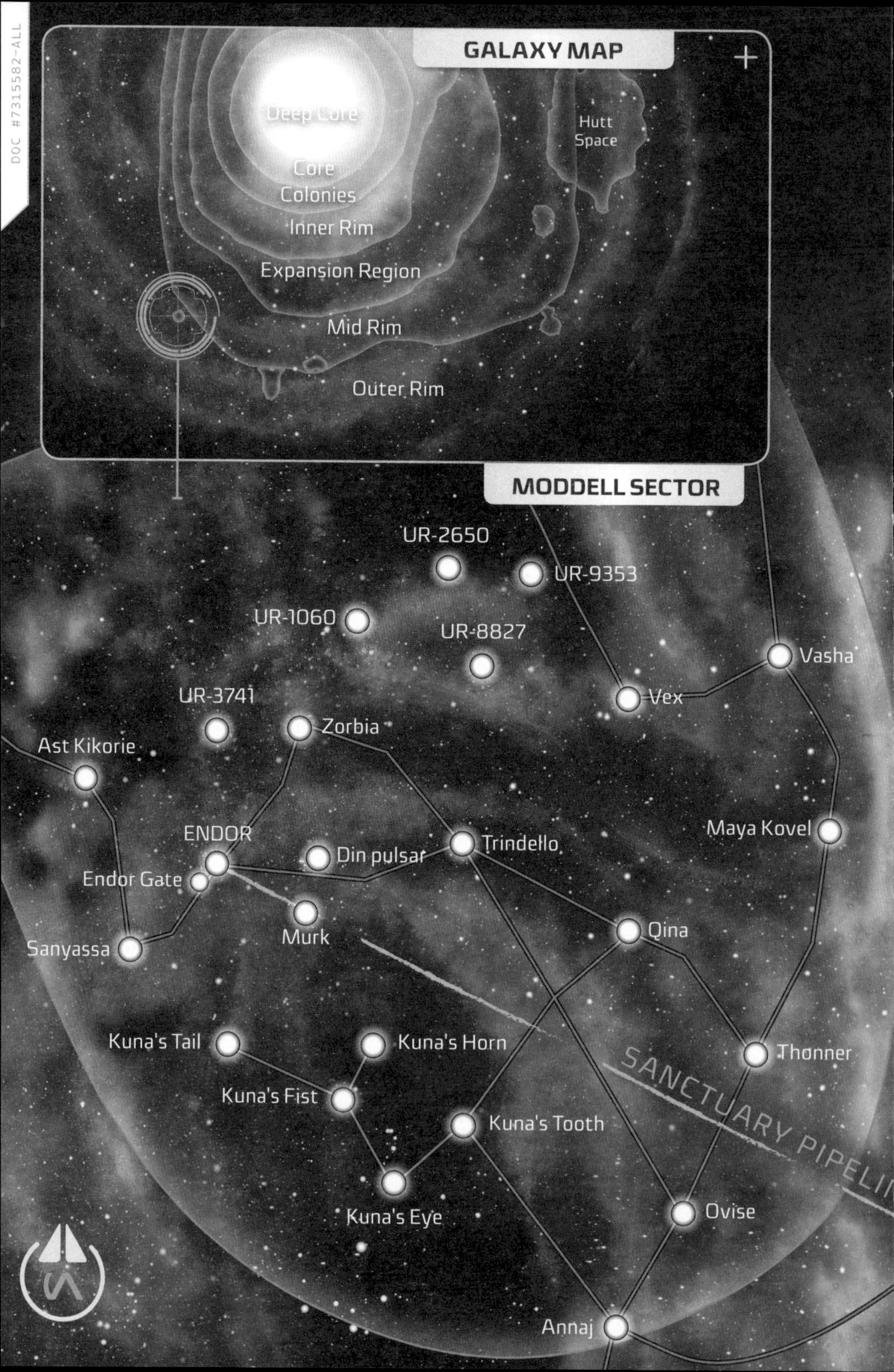

GALAXY MAP

Deep Core
Core
Colonies
Inner Rim
Expansion Region
Mid Rim
Outer Rim
Hutt
Space

MODDELL SECTOR

UR-2650
UR-9353
UR-1060
UR-8827
Vasha
Vex
UR-3741
Zorbia
Ast Kikorie
Maya Kovel
ENDOR
Din pulsar
Trindello
Endor Gate
Murk
Qina
Sanyassa
Kuna's Tail
Kuna's Horn
Thonner
SANCTUARY PIPELI
Kuna's Fist
Kuna's Tooth
Kuna's Eye
Ovise
Annaj

DOC #7315582-ALL

MODDELL SECTOR NAVIGATION
SPECIAL REPORT, AS REQUESTED
FILED BY: Cpl. Ractivelle, Stardust unit, Alliance SpecForces

The Empire couldn't have picked a trickier knothole. I know the hyperspace terrain near the southern seam better than anyone, and it's a wonder Imperial scouts ever made it to Endor at all. Don't ask me how an Imperial construction crew followed them, or how they can keep funneling supplies there day after day.

The easiest way into the Moddell sector for our fleet is the Spar Trade Route, but that ends at Annaj where an Imperial picket will almost certainly be guarding the reversion point. The Houche Run will take you the rest of the way until you hit the hopscotch approach leading past the Monsua and the Din Nebula.

If you're planning a surprise attack, forget it. Traversing the Moddell is slow going. You'll be spotted, I guarantee it.

The Alliance actually exploited this same type of hyperspace wilderness when establishing safeworlds and supply caches. Helpful when you don't have to get in or out in a hurry.
—Holdo

END DOCUMENT

CLASSIFIED DOCUMENT—CLEARANCE LEVEL: 

HARINAR/MADINE PROG42087

RI 036-SP16
HYPERSPATIAL UPDATE: STRAIGHT SHOT FROM SULLUST
TO: GENERAL MADINE
FROM: MAJOR HARINAR

Look at the line on this map. Fast, clear, and straight. This is what the Empire is calling the Sanctuary Pipeline.

It runs directly between Sullust on the Rimma and Endor in Moddell. That's how the Empire is doing it. That's how they've shunted thousands of cargo barges to a construction site without our agents on Annaj seeing a thing.

CONTINUED

HARINAR/MADINE PROG42087

How is this route not on the charts, you ask? Ah, that's why I'm the one authoring this report, not some vapechaser. It's technology, my dear general!

You see, a hyperlane existed here once, but galactic drift washed it out of alignment. Gravitational muddying is correctable through technology if you have exceptionally deep pockets, with S-thread boosters to prop up a collapsed hyperlane assuming you know where to place them. My team believes the Empire has done exactly that with the Sanctuary Pipeline.

Now that we have its coordinates, we know how to ride it. Think about it: Imps are sitting around waiting for another cargo shipment, and here comes the Rebel fleet dropping onto their doorstep instead. Won't they be surprised!

Could the Order be u this technolo now? We h yet to figu out how they're navigating the Unknown Regions. -Statura

END DOCUMENT

DOC #7244566-ALL

TO: CMDR MOTHMA

FROM: ADMIRAL ACKBAR

SUBJ: FLEET STAGING AREA

In light of Harinar's discovery, Sullust is the only acceptable fleet staging area. We must launch from there if we are to travel the Sanctuary Pipeline, yet such a rendezvous is unlikely to betray our intentions. We have already struck Sullust once during Operation Ringbreaker and it is wholly believable we might return for another engagement.

As soon as the Death Star is gone, the fleet will return to free Sullust. You can tell Councilor Tevv he has my word on that.

And we did, though it may have taken months instead of days. When the fighting ended, Mon Mothma and I escorted Sian Tevv into the government center for his ceremonial inauguration. Admiral Ack

CRACKEN TO MON MOTHMA

We've seen this type of behavior from Leia Organa before. Remember when she broke Dodonna's quarantine on Yavin 4 to rescue Alderaanian survivors?

And more recently, she compromised Operation Yellow Moon by warning the rebels who responded to the diversionary beacons in the Corva sector. Yes, she succeeded (eliminating a Star Destroyer and capturing an Imperial shuttle in the process). But we can't give a rogue element free rein within our organization.

In my view, Draven's concerns are valid.

DOC #7311541-ALL

TO: GENERAL CRACKEN

FROM: GENERAL DRAVEN

SUBJ: HAN SOLO TATOOINE EXTRACTION: MISSION IS NOT ACTIVE

Is the Princess running her own op?

Don't get me wrong, I'm sorry we lost Solo too. But we have to know when to move on. Fett is one of the best bounty hunters in the galaxy and Jabba is untouchable. And carbon freeze? Survival rates are low under the best conditions, and an industrial gas refinery probably isn't hitting those numbers.

I've made this all very clear, in response to multiple inquiries. And yet my department is still pulling reports for Leia Organa. Some requests from just this morning:

- Architectural specs for Jabba's palace on file with Mos Eisley Territorial Planning Authority
- Eyewitness descriptions of palace interior, collected by Tac-Com from interviews with musicians and entertainers (transcripts "Rystall" and "Rappertunie")
- Dossiers on prominent courtesans and hangers-on in

CONTINUED

DOC #7311541-ALL

Jabba's court (largest datafile Ephant Mon, 22 partial bios)

- 18-month log of Jabba's movements, including offworld trips and recreational sorties to Tatooine's Dune Sea
- Blueprints for the Ubrikkian Industries LO-KD57 (stock model of Jabba's luxury sail barge)
- Full text of Ebenn Q3 Baobab's *Easy Ubese Phrase Book*

I can't deny a request from a senior member of Alliance command. But I'm not willing to send my agents on a suicide mission. Leia Organa hasn't asked for that, however, nor has she asked Onoran for SpecForces personnel.

So I ask again—is the Princess running her own op?

END

CRACKEN TO MON MOTHMA

I'm forwarding this one as well. I suspect it's related.

I must ask. Is Skywalker working with the Princess on a rescue mission? I can't blame them for helping a friend, but you should know that Intelligence reacts poorly to being kept in the dark.

DOC #7325662-ALL

TO: GENERAL DODONNA, STARFIGHTER COMMAND

FROM: COMMANDER ANTILLES, ROGUE LEADER

SUBJ: COMMANDER SKYWALKER

General, I will be continuing as commander of Rogue Squadron for the immediate future. Commander Skywalker is extending his leave to focus on personal matters.

Further requests concerning this matter should be directed to Commander Skywalker. As you can imagine, Rogue Squadron's upcoming mission schedule requires my full attention.

HENDRI UNDERHOLT

It's as we suspected. Leia and Chewbacca are with the *Falcon* on Tatooine, but they're not ready to move just yet.

MON MOTHMA

Her thinking behind this is utterly enigmatic. She hasn't told us anything.

HENDRI UNDERHOLT

We just need to keep the channels open. And also stop well-meaning experts from mucking things up. As for the rest . . . we must trust in her.

MON MOTHMA

Every nerve is screaming at me to send in the fleet.

CYNABAR'S INFONET

Always Bet on the Big CYN

What Just Happened on Tatooine?

Tatooine—It's chaos in the Arkanis sector, with multiple sources reporting the assassination of Jabba the Hutt on Tatooine.

We still don't know what to think. Some are swearing that Jabba died in the explosion of his sail barge, with the culprits variously identified as the Alliance, the Empire, a rival crime syndicate, rebellious slaves, and even the planet's native "Sand People."

Other sources aren't sweating Jabba's survival. They have assured Cynabar's that Jabba's operations are unaffected and that the rimward Corellian Run will experience no disruption in smuggling traffic.

Who to believe? The truth will come out eventually, but don't look to the Hutt Council for answers. Cynabar's will keep supplying live updates from our contacts in the field, so come back often for the latest news.

FOR THE BETTER PART OF A YEAR, JABBA'S RIVALS IN THE RED KEY RAIDERS CONTINUED TO TAKE THE BLAME FOR HIS DEATH. —MATT

DOC #7511303-ALL

TO: CMDR MOTHMA

FROM: ADMIRAL ACKBAR

SUBJ: FLEET COMPOSITION AND STRENGTH

I am drawing in critical fleet elements in preparation for our assemblage above Sullust. For the Endor attack, we will be much better armed than we were at Scarif. It appears that planning and preparation have some value after all!

CONTINUED

STARSHIP SQUADRONS

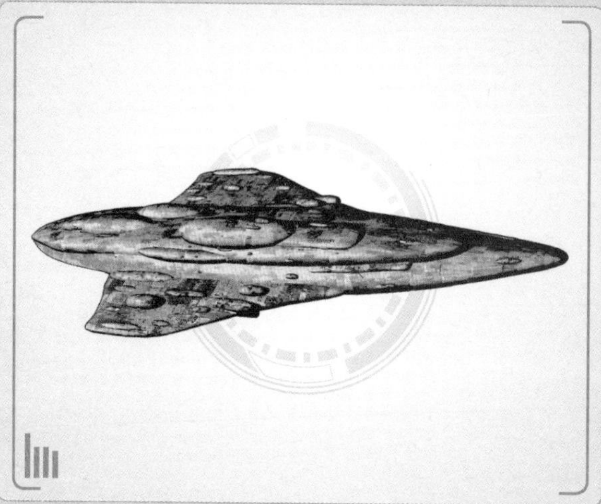

MC80 STAR CRUISER

MANUFACTURER: Mon Calamari Shipyards
LENGTH: 1,200 meters
ARMAMENT: Turbolaser cannons, ion cannons, tractor beam projectors, missile tubes; up to 10 squadrons of starfighters
CREW: over 5,000
ROLE: Command, carrier, capital ship engagement

CONFIRMED SHIPS: *Home One*, *Nautilian*, *Liberty*, *Amalthea* (pending hyerdrive repair)
TENTATIVE SHIPS: *Restoration*, *Freedom's Run*

The Alliance's bunker busters must not have been in service yet. Within a year they starte[d] seeing actio[n]. -Hold[o]

PELTA-CLASS FRIGATE

MANUFACTURER: Kuat Drive Yards
LENGTH: 282 meters
ARMAMENT: Turbolasers, point-defense laser cannons
CREW: 900
ROLE: Communications, medical, anti-starfighter, fire support

EF76 NEBULON-B ESCORT FRIGATE

MANUFACTURER: Kuat Drive Yards
LENGTH: 300 meters
ARMAMENT: Turbolasers, laser cannons, tractor beam projectors, torpedo launchers (variant)
CREW: 850
ROLE: Carrier, anti-starfighter, medical, bombardment

ANTI-STARFIGHTER? YOU'RE NOT KIDDING! THESE THINGS ARE A COUPLE GENERATIONS FROM NEW, BUT IT'S PRETTY COMMON FOR ONE TO BE PACKING A DOZEN LASER CANNONS, A DOZEN TURBOLASERS, AND A COUPLE OF MISSILE LAUNCHERS. NO THANKS. -POE

CR90 CORVETTE

MANUFACTURER: Corellian Engineering Corporation
LENGTH: 150 meters
ARMAMENT: Turbolaser cannons, dual turbolaser turrets
CREW: 165
ROLE: Fast attack

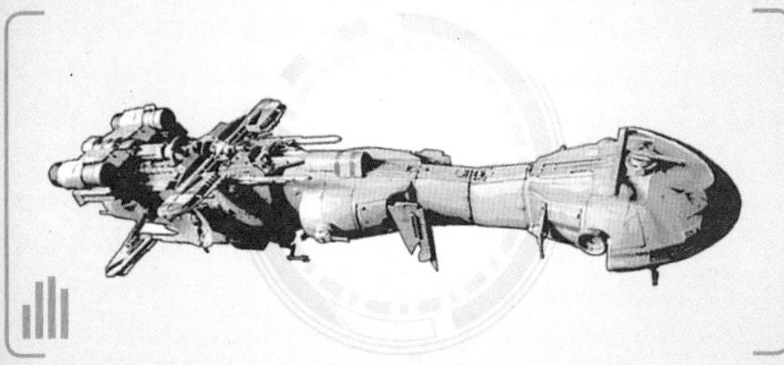

BRAHA'TOK-CLASS GUNSHIP

MANUFACTURER: Dornean Braha'ket Fleetworks Conglomerate
LENGTH: 90 meters
ARMAMENT: Double turbolaser cannons, concussion missile launchers
CREW: 75
ROLE: Fast attack, bombardment

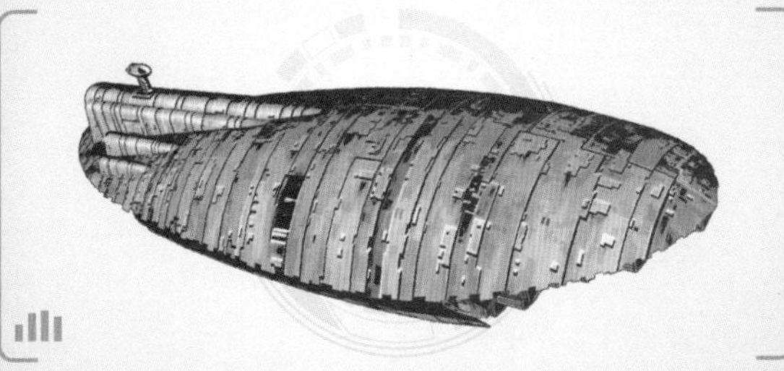

GR-75 MEDIUM TRANSPORT

MANUFACTURER: Gallofree Yards
LENGTH: 90 meters
ARMAMENT: Twin laser cannon turrets
CREW: 6
ROLE: Resupply, communications, rescue, fire support

STARFIGHTER SQUADRONS

A-WINGS: Starfight Screen; DS Attack Run
B-WINGS: Anti-Captial Bomber
X-WINGS: Starfight Screen; DS Attack Run
Y-WINGS: Anti-Captial Bomber

NOT A FAN OF MIXED-DESIGN SQUADRONS, BUT I'M NOT HERE TO TELL THE ADMIRAL HIS BUSINESS.
-POE

No, you are not, Lieutenant.
Admiral Ackbar

NOTE: All single type specialty squadrons will be engaged. Other squadrons will be mixed, to better prepare us for an uncertain battlefield.

ADDENDUM: ACKBAR TO MON MOTHMA

Commander, a new development. We may have more ships at our disposal, assuming the claims of our newest recruit are more than just mist.

TO:
Admiral Ackbar
Alliance to Restore the Republic
***Home One*, Alliance Fleet**

Admiral,
I can see that you've been working every angle to build up your armada before the big battle. If you will allow me, I may have angles that you haven't considered yet.

I recently stepped down as administrator of a major tibanna mine. My duties there—as well as jobs I've held among less distinguished company—introduced me to unconventional friends in interesting places.

All I ask is that you have a look. If the Alliance is interested, I'll make the introductions.

X4 Gunship

MANUFACTURER: Incom Corporation
ARMAMENT: Laser cannons, light laser cannon turrets
Note: These are the operational prototypes from the X4 line. They're working a Mining Guild patrol near Kessel. Some exterior carbon scoring, but they're still in solid shape.

The Corellian gunships were there at Endor. The Kesselian X4s, too. It didn't even take much convincing. Lots of people wanted to hurt the Empire. —Leia

Corellian gunship (DP20 Frigate)

MANUFACTURER: Corellian Engineering Corporation
ARMAMENT: Double turbolaser cannons, quad laser cannons, concussion missile launchers
Note: They're small, they're fast, and they hit hard. A group of Alderaanian exiles has four of these gunships. I know where to find them.

Aftermarket YT freighters

MANUFACTURER: Corellian Engineering Corporation
ARMAMENT: Variable
Note: I know the *Home One*'s crewers appreciate the *Millennium Falcon* because I've had the pleasure of giving the grand tour to more than one student of fine workmanship. You have an open invitation, Admiral.

Let me be clear, no freighter will ever match the *Falcon*. But you'd be surprised how well some of them handle in combat. Everything from the YT-450 to the YT-2400 can be had for a price, crews included. And the list of weapon configurations runs longer than the list carried by a Brentaali sommelier.

Awaiting your reply,

Lando Calrissian

Lando Calrissian

DOC #7566225-ALL

TO: ADMIRAL ACKBAR

FROM: CMDR MOTHMA

SUBJ: DEATH STAR REACTOR RUN: STARFIGHTER RECOMMENDATION NEEDED

Admiral, you've seen General Madine's analysis. He believes we can take out the Death Star with proton torpedoes delivered at close range.

Our success will come down to our starfighters. Who have you identified to lead this attack? Will Luke accept a role within Starfighter Command?

ACKBAR TO MON MOTHMA

I have another, more unexpected recommendation. Although my experience with the human is limited, he has impressed me within a very short time. The endorsements of Ensign Deltura and Nien Nunb (our Sullustan resistance liaison) washed away my clinging doubts.

HENDRI UNDERHOLT

That was quite an experience. The things you get me into, Commander.

MON MOTHMA

Did you secure a commitment from Calrissian?

HENDRI UNDERHOLT

Yes, I did. Ackbar tried to appeal to his honor but when that didn't work, he went straight to money. Lando's more complicated than that, and frankly he was a little offended.

MON MOTHMA

Thank you for turning things around. So we have our Gold Leader?

HENDRI UNDERHOLT

For the Battle of Endor, yes, but I see more than that. Lando would be an unstoppable diplomat and an enormous asset to our cause. Problem is, he bores easily.

I regret that General Calrissian didn't remain in the service. Admiral Ackbar

Even at that rank, the pay rate can't compare to the private sector. –Statura

DOC #7866312-ALL

TO: MON MOTHMA

FROM: GEN DRAVEN, ALLIANCE INTELLIGENCE

SUBJ: UNCERTAINTY RE: INTEL VERIFICATION

Commander— This is worth a look, even though you've seen this argument before.

Despite what you see in this transcript, Intelligence's recommendation is the same as before. Endor is a go.

EXCERPTED BRIEFING ROOM RECORDINGS:
HOME ONE, ALLIANCE INTELLIGENCE

SR. ANALYST AISHA FREITAS: Yes, it's just a feeling. But my intuition is borne out by the implausibility of the data. A surprisingly vulnerable Death Star and a visiting Emperor Palpatine, all occurring within a window that gives the Alliance time to mount a large-scale attack?

COL. HAXAN DELTO: Yes, and?

FREITAS: I think it's a trap.

DELTO: I participated in a very similar conversation years ago during the preparations for the Battle of Yavin. I was in favor of the attack. Or was I against it?

FREITAS: Yes, I'm familiar with the counterargument. Ontological objections shouldn't be hauled out to dismiss legitimate concerns. What if we're wrong? It could be a disaster for the Alliance.

DELTO: Taking things back to Yavin—if we had held back in that moment, we would have squandered the greatest Intelligence coup in a generation.

FREITAS: I know I don't have the rank to make my voice heard among the higher-ups.

DELTO: Well that isn't what I want you to—

FREITAS: You have to tell them. I don't care if you agree with me. I don't care about winning this argument. Just tell them.

I don't recall seeing this report. I don't think it would have made a difference. Only a major crisis could have slowed the momentum of our preparations.
—Leia

CONTINUED

DOC #7866312-ALL

DELTO/CRACKEN PROG42087

CLASSIFIED DOCUMENT—CLEARANCE LEVEL:

RI 040-X08

ENERGY SHIELD? ARE WE PLANNING FOR THIS?

TO: GEN. CRACKEN

FROM: COL. DELTO

Honestly did anyone think the Empire was going to leave its prize completely exposed?

Take a second look at the Bothan data. Now look at data-sector NI-56-NA-357-AC. That's the energy shield. Just like the one at Scarif, but projected from Endor's forest moon. Remote power source, remote projection, and it completely envelops the construction sphere.

We can't fly starfighters through that. Our only option is to switch off the energy shield at its source.

END DOCUMENT

CLASSIFIED DOCUMENT—CLEARANCE LEVEL:

MADINE/MOTHMA PROG42133

RI 044-X08

STRIKE TEAM: ENDOR FOREST MOON

TO: COMMANDER MOTHMA

FROM: GENERAL MADINE

Dealing with the shield, however, is hardly an impossible task. By interrupting the projector or destroying it outright, we will give our starfighters time to penetrate the Death Star's inner core and detonate its reactor.

Taking out the shield projector is a ground assault mission—classic Special Forces. I recommend selected members of the Pathfinders and the 32nd Commando Unit.

- Maj. Bren Derlin
- Lt. Caluan Ematt
- Sgt. Judder Page
- Sgt. Kes Dameron
- Cpl. Tuck Tyrell
- Cpl. Frorral

HEY! THAT'S MY DAD! AND MOM WOULD HAVE BEEN PREPPING HER X-WING RIGHT AROUND THIS TIME. -POE

CONTINUED

I THOUGHT I MIGHT GET A MENTION. DERLIN AND PAGE HANDLED THE BULK OF THE MISSION, AND FRORRAL DIDN'T MAKE THE SQUAD AT ALL. CAME DOWN WITH A FUR RASH, SHE SAID. - EMATT

We have an Imperial *Lambda*-class shuttle at our disposal, captured by Leia Organa during Operation Yellow Moon. The shuttle's code clearances should give us safe passage through the orbital cordon.

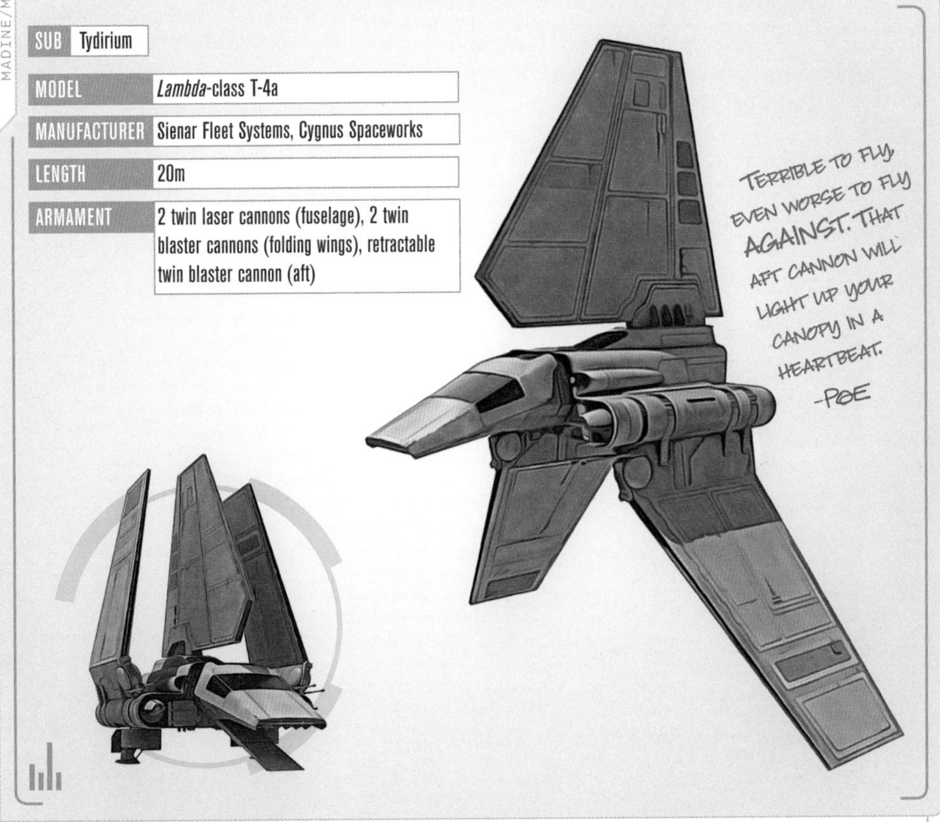

SUB	Tydirium
MODEL	*Lambda*-class T-4a
MANUFACTURER	Sienar Fleet Systems, Cygnus Spaceworks
LENGTH	20m
ARMAMENT	2 twin laser cannons (fuselage), 2 twin blaster cannons (folding wings), retractable twin blaster cannon (aft)

END DOCUMENT

MADINE TO MON MOTHMA

Rest assured that all commandos assigned to the Endor strike team will be experts in wilderness reconnaissance. Seertay literally wrote the book on this, and she was the soul of the Pathfinders. We lost her during Operation Cobalt.

COMBAT TACTICS:
JUNGLE ENVIRONMENTS
ALLIANCE SPECIAL FORCES

By Colonel Anna Seertay, Alliance Pathfinders

Jungle ecosystems are common across settled space. They can be identified by heavy vegetation, high rainfall, and tropical climates. Forested environments thrive at lower temperatures, but are governed by similar combat principles.

Know Where You're Going.
This is the vital principle underlying jungle operations. The enemy can't easily find you beneath the tree canopy, but you're getting a bad hand in return:

1  SENSOR INTERFERENCE

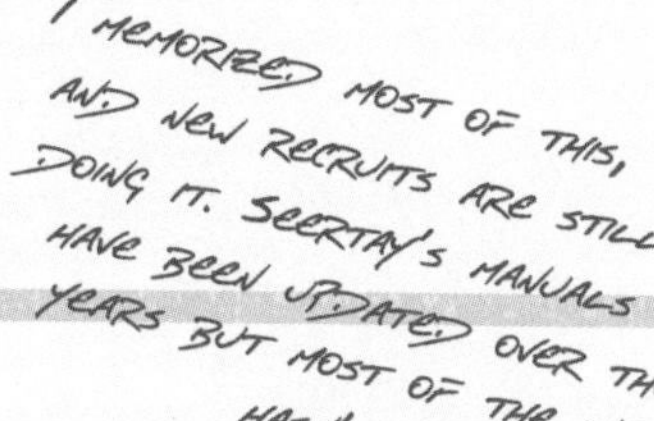

2  LIKELIHOOD OF TRAPS OR AMBUSHES

3  UNFAMILIAR WILDLIFE NESTING GROUNDS

4  FOLIAGE THAT OBSCURES SKY, REDUCING ILLUMINATION AND PREVENTING STELLAR NAVIGATION

5  SUDDEN RAINFALL THAT CAN WASH AWAY TERRAIN MARKERS

There's little you can do about those problems once you've made landfall, so stack things in your favor from the start. Always:

- Obtain current charts, especially aerial or orbital reconnaissance
- Carry multiple terrain trackers
- Rely on treelines and ridgelines for easy visual navigation
- Avoid roads, trails, and streambeds due to increased likelihood of surveillance
- Identify natural clearings that can be used for message transmission or resupply drops

Get There in One Piece.

When traveling, take up a three-column formation with security teams at point and rear. If threatened, the flanks can easily expand outward and become a full-perimeter formation (fig. A).

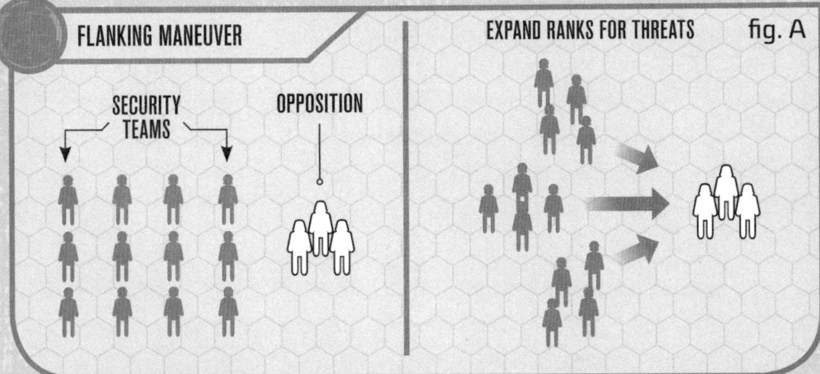

Combat engineers and special-weapons flamethrowers should be shielded in the center of the formation (fig. B). Call them up when you need to deal with enemy fortifications.

MOTHMA | JOURNAL ENTRY

Operation Yellow Moon was just the start. We need to stage more distractions to keep the Empire in the dark. That means continuing this absurd theater, and sending soldiers to their deaths for objectives that are likely to prove meaningless.

It must be this way. If we ease off now, our Endor preparations will stand out like a burning beacon.

People will continue to die on my orders. I can only hope to make their deaths count for something.

Fight to END the fight, not to prolong it. Sometimes it seems brutal, but it allows you to live with the results. —Leia

CLASSIFIED DOCUMENT—CLEARANCE LEVEL:

CRACKEN/MOTHMA PROG42009

RI 124-C18

DIVERSIONARY CAMPAIGN: YOUR ROLE

TO: COMMANDER MOTHMA

FROM: GENERAL CRACKEN

Our preparations for the Endor attack will be noticed. There's no way around it. Our counter is to make equally intriguing moves elsewhere, leaving the Empire torn on what to focus on next.

At this time, the best card we can play is the possibility of your arrest.

We do it by creating a data trail outlining your impending visit to an Alliance-friendly world—someplace far removed from Endor, with no overlapping jurisdictions or reporting hierarchies. A false timetable will dangle the lure of intercept and capture.

You will not actually make the journey, and your security will not be at risk. It will be enough to make the Empire chase a data ghost.

MON MOTHMA TO GENERAL CRACKEN

You're trying to protect me, and I appreciate that. But your scenario won't fool Imperial agents watching over spaceport arrivals. We need bodies on the ground to help sell the illusion.

I will make the journey, along with the bodyguards and escorts that typically accompany a visiting head of state.

GENERAL CRACKEN TO MON MOTHMA

I'd rather you didn't. But you're correct that a party moving from port to port will keep the trackers busy. Give me some time to come up with a plan. I'll be in contact soon with a recommendation.

CLASSIFIED DOCUMENT—CLEARANCE LEVEL: 

CRACKEN/MOTHMA PROG42215

RI 098-D03
ENDOR MISDIRECTION: DURKTEEL
TO: COMMANDER MOTHMA
FROM: GENERAL CRACKEN

Intelligence is recommending Durkteel for your mission. Its position in the northern Mid Rim is as far from Endor as we can get, and in the eyes of Imperial analysts it is probable that we might visit Durkteel in a bid to reclaim our lost holdings.

SUPPORTING POINTS:

- The Alliance abandoned Durkteel during the Mid Rim retreat. The sloppiness of our evacuation of the Tak-Beam complex lends itself to the interpretation that we may have mistakenly left valuable intel behind.

CONTINUED

- The Empire has neglected to reoccupy Durkteel. The planet currently has no garrison or orbital picket.
- Durkteel's position near major hyperlanes and the loyalty of its native Saurin provide further justification for why it might host a high-ranking summit.

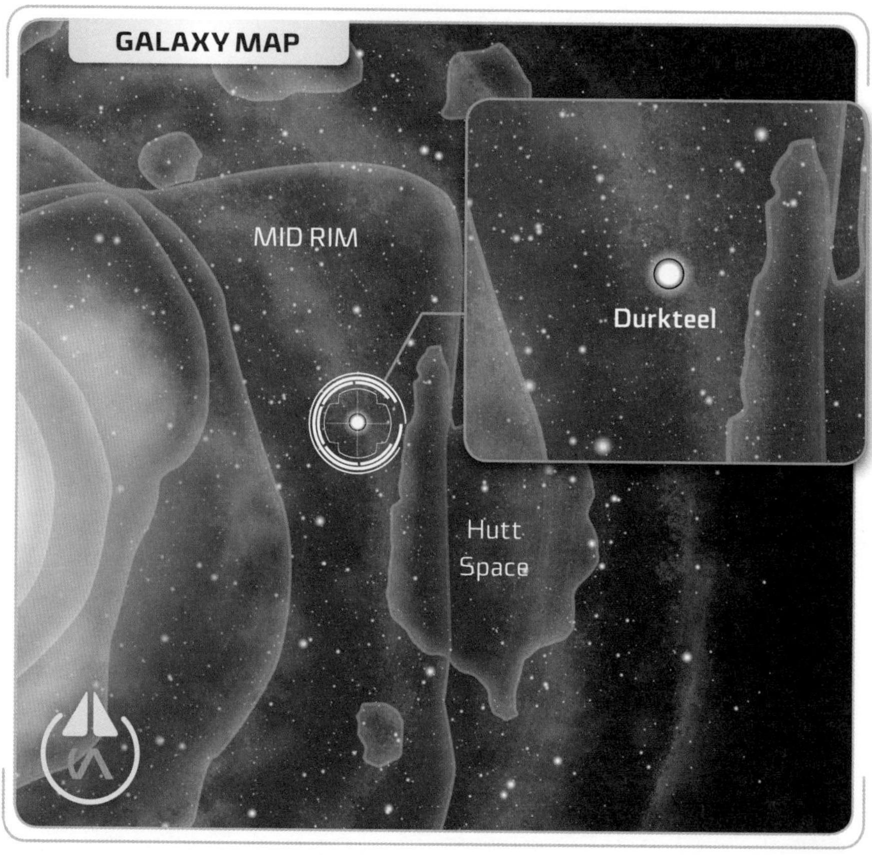

NOTE: Though the Durkteel mission is a ruse, we can accomplish several practical outcomes by slicing the BRT supercomputer at Tak-Beam. These include:

- Passive telemetry of hyperjumps and reversions from the Roche node
- Assessment of Imperial military readiness in the Near Perlemian

CRACKEN/MOTHMA PROG42215

- Data shredding of Alliance passkey algorithm [52tempoR-22spatio]
- Dossiers of Saurin resistance officers active on Durkteel

Rumors of your trip will be leaked in advance. We want to draw the Empire's attention but not provoke an immediate response. You will be in and out of the Durkteel system in less than twenty-four hours, so by the time Imperial investigators take action you will already be on your way back to the fleet.

I VAGUELY RECALL DURKTEEL, AND TAK-BEAM. BUT I VIVIDLY RECALL THE AFTERMATH. - EMATT

END DOCUMENT

HENDRI UNDERHOLT

I heard the news from Hostis. You're not seriously going to Durkteel in person?

MON MOTHMA

The Empire must not conclude that Endor is our target. And Intelligence has leaked the news of my trip already.

HENDRI UNDERHOLT

You can't risk it. The price on your head is in the millions.

MON MOTHMA

I'm not needed at Endor. I'm not military like Ackbar or Madine.
But I'm a big target, and the Empire watches my movements. This is how I can help.
It's a short turnaround and I'll have Special Forces guarding me all the way.

HENDRI UNDERHOLT

Let me do it.

MON MOTHMA

I'm sorry, but . . . how do you propose to do that?

HENDRI UNDERHOLT

I'm your closest aide. They know that. I travel with you and they know that too. If I move into contested territory accompanied by a bunch of soldiers and bodyguards—you're telling me they wouldn't boost that straight up to the Intelligence director?

MON MOTHMA

There's a risk.

HENDRI UNDERHOLT

A risk that the bodyguards and soldiers aren't already facing? Let me do this.

CYNABAR'S INFONET

Always Bet on the Big CYN

Are the Rebels Romancing the Mid Rim All Over Again?

They've been humiliated once, but could they turn things around the second time? After abandoning the Mid Rim when the Empire pushed back, the Alliance reportedly has its eyes on the region once more.

According to sources, a high-ranking Alliance chief is en route to the Perlemian. Planets such as Trasse, Durkteel, Jeyell, and Ord Tiddell have surfaced as potential sites for a rebel summit or for the establishment of a new planet-based headquarters.

Cynabar readers in the Mid Rim—we want to hear from you. What's going on up there? Is the Alliance planning another ground war? And if they're hiring mercenaries, what's the going rate?

DOC #8144260-ALL

TO: HENDRI UNDERHOLT

FROM: MON MOTHMA

SUBJ: FINAL PREPARATIONS

Hendri, enclosed is the draft of the address I plan to deliver to our forces on the day of the attack. Please store it with the other documents in the archive. I hope it will have historical significance, but such a fate will ultimately be determined by the actions of others.

I note that you're scheduled to depart for Durkteel at 0600. Though your mission is not without risk, I am grateful you will be far away from the center of the storm.

I need to deliver inspiration but all I can think about right now are eventualities. Comm silence means we won't speak again until your squad is recalled. I want to tell you that I am honored by the sacrifices you have made for the Alliance, and how proud I am of the leader you have become. Thank you for your friendship.

And hurry back. Win or lose, we have a lot of work to do.

Fellow Fighters of the Alliance

Today, you will undertake the most important action against the Empire since the Battle of Yavin. At Yavin, we fought with our backs to the wall, yet we triumphed against impossible odds.

Today, we are the ones in control. Today, we bring the fight to our enemy. Today, it is the Empire who will feel the shock of surprise. Our victory will be hard-won, but it *must* be won.

We have achieved much since our fighting units came together under the banner of the Rebel Alliance. Through the dark times and the lean times our resolve has never faltered. Our will is strong, and our wish is to put this war behind us. We had no choice but to wage war against the Empire, but it is our moral duty to bring it to a swift end.

Today, we are ready to fight for freedom. Today, we stand before our greatest triumph.

Without victory there is no tomorrow, but today, victory will be ours. Good luck, and may the Force be with you.

Library of Congress Cataloging-in-Publication Data available.

ISBN: 978-1-7856-5875-4

The Rebel Files: Collected Intelligence of the Alliance is published by Titan Books
A division of Titan Publishing Group Ltd., 144 Southwark St.,
London, SE1 0UP
www.titanbooks.com

Published by arrangement with becker&mayer! an Imprint of the Quarto Group
www.QuartoKnows.com

Design: Sam Dawson
Editorial: Delia Greve
Production: Tom Miller

17 18 19 20 21 5 4 3 2 1

Manufactured in China 12/17

MIX
Paper from responsible sources
FSC® C017606

Author: Daniel Wallace

Illustrations by: Aaron Riley: Pages 2–3, 48–49, 96–97, 140–141; Adrián Rodriguez: Pages 16, 46, 76, 113; Chris Reiff: Page 127; Chris Trevas: Pages 42, 56, 74; Diogo Costa: Pages 23, 63, 72, 75, 80–81, 108, 126, 130; Giorgio Baroni: Pages 9, 10, 11, 35, 43, 67, 68, 110, 114; Isaac Hannaford: Pages 7, 15; Joe Corroney: Pages 25, 51, 52, 59, 105, 160, 161; Maciej Rebisz: Pages 33, 162, 163; Randall Mackey: Pages 20, 21, 24, 27, 28, 29, 31

Did you enjoy this book? We love to hear from our readers.
Please e-mail us at: readerfeedback@titanemail.com
or write to Reader Feedback at the above address.

305234